Surviving
the Siege of Beirut

a personal account

Lina Mikdadi

45

ONYX PRESS

Onyx Press Ltd.
86 Lauriston Road
London E9 7HA

ISBN 0 906383 21 8 (cased)
ISBN 0 906383 22 6 (paperback)

Acknowledgements to Bantam Books for permission to publish extracts
from Ezer Weizman, *The Battle for Peace.*

Set in Baskerville
Typeset by H. Hems, Chilmark, Wilts.
Printed by The Russell Press Ltd., Nottingham

*Woe betide you who make your companions drink the
    outpouring of your wrath,
    making them drunk, that you may watch their naked
    orgies!*
*Drink deep draughts of shame, not of glory;
    you too shall drink until you stagger.*
*The cup in the Lord's right hand is passed to you,
    and your shame will exceed your glory.*
*The violence done to Lebanon shall sweep over you,
    the havoc done to its beasts shall break your own spirit,
    because of bloodshed and violence done in the land,
    to the city and all its inhabitants.*

Habakkuk (2)
The Old Testament

This book is dedicated to my city and its heroic inhabitants, those who stayed; to my daughters Leyla and Rasha, who survived the siege; and to my nephews and nieces Marwan, Catherine, Ridha, Hania, Richard, Husni and Alana Les Moyler who never saw the siege. May they all grow and live by principles and ideals, whatever these may be.

By the same author
Survival in Beirut: a diary of civil war

CHAPTER 1

Today is July 10th, 1982—or is it July 11th? I don't know any more. My mind is not fixed on the present but on the past as I try to travel back in time and remember if there was ever a happy moment in our lives.

Right now I'm lying in bed, half-dressed, half-ready to rush down eight floors to the shelter below if I get the chance. The scene outside is apocalyptic and the noise is deafening. They tell you that you get used to it, but bombing is bombing. The closer its gets to you the more you panic.

Were there ever happier times—in my childhood, in my adolescence, in my youth? These days I keep having recurrent dreams of the time when I was a child of six in Jaffa. I remember one day when my only care in the world was to hold on to a large watermelon I had taken from one of the trucks carrying the fruit from my father's fields. My elder brother and I lugged it around all day, this prized possession, until finally the inevitable happened and it slipped from our grasp and split open in the stone courtyard. The red pulp splashed out messily, the shiny black seeds spraying on to the ground.

Another vivid memory is of a fifteen year-old girl with long auburn braids who played and played in a lovely house surrounded by a garden in Beirut until the day she was told her mother had died. She hadn't even known her mother was dying and she loved her so very much, this wonderful woman with the huge green eyes who was gone forever, leaving behind dreams and a yearning for happiness.

My mind wanders back to the immediate past, to the summer of 1977 which was in retrospect a lovely summer. After two years of hell on earth, I decided to take my children to the mountains and make believe that nothing had happened. My husband Nabil left for Europe by car. He too wanted to put behind him all that had taken place in Lebanon in 1975-76, the two years of civil war with their bombings, kidnappings, fear and hatred, their unanswered questions and their unsolved problems. Who needed answers any more when you could have Ainab and the peace offered by this breathtakingly beautiful village in the mountains of the Chouf?

My daughters Leyla (now six) and Rasha (four) and I could look down at Beirut from our garden and really pretend that

5

nothing had taken place in the half-destroyed capital of Lebanon that was effectively partitioned. In the summer resorts, the only reminder of those two years were the Syrian checkpoints on the main roads.

One day that summer I was taking Leyla, Rasha and some of their little friends on a tour of neighbouring villages when I was stopped at one of the barricades. Courtesy was a word that did not exist in the vocabulary of the Syrian soldiers.

'Open all the windows,' one of the three soldiers who surrounded our small car said rudely. I did so promptly.

'Your identity card,' said another, while the third opened my bag, searched it and threw it into the car. The first took my identity card, examined it, turned it upside down, looked at the photograph and then at me.

'Your children's identity cards!' he ordered.

'I don't have them, I only carry mine,' I replied.

'What do you mean, you don't have them? You must. It's the rule.'

'They're only children.'

'What kind of an answer is this? Don't you know the regulations? All people must carry their identity cards.'

'Well, I don't have them, but I am ready to go and get them if you insist,' I said.

'All right, but the children will wait for you here.'

'What?'

'You heard me. Children, get out!'

'Nobody's getting out,' I snapped. Anger welled up in me, anger mingled with disbelief and fear. Two of the soldiers seemed to be enjoying the scene tremendously, while the third remained stern and adamant.

'Listen, woman,' he said, 'What proof do I have that these are your daughters and you haven't kidnapped them?'

'Ask them; go ahead, ask them.'

He turned to Rasha: 'Who is this woman?' There was no answer. 'Who is this woman?' he repeated.

'I don't want to tell you,' Rasha said coyly.

I turned to her: 'Tell him who I am. What's your name? Who are you?' I didn't know what I was saying any more. But Rasha shook her straight black hair; she wasn't about to give in. Leyla, to whom I turned for help, was busy examining the cannon installed at the check-point. It took the soldier ten minutes to

6

abandon his prey on the condition that I would not go on to the next village. 'Go back to where you came from. This way I'll know that you're not kidnapping them,' he said condescendingly. I thanked my lucky stars: that was a good day, I had fallen on an indulgent soldier.

Thereafter, we restricted our excursions to the streets of Ainab, but we needed no more than that—we had peace. That summer I discovered that looking at olive trees and pine trees was more soothing than all the valium in the world. We picknicked in the woods, played hide and seek, planted tomato seeds which never grew for lack of water, made bonfires, and I wrote a novel. It took me three months to put the final touches to the book that was going to take the world by storm. It's still stashed away in a drawer; I never looked at it again.

Soon the leaves started to fall and it was time to go back to reality; school was about to start. I didn't want to return to Beirut. During those three months in the mountains I had listened to no news, had read no papers, and had seen no one. I had been very happily quiet and at peace.

Beirut again—noisy, dirty, miserable capital in distress. I still wanted to forget, to ignore the misery around me: the pitted streets and uprooted sidewalks, the damaged buildings, the posh apartment blocks turned into mass havens for the thousands of poor people from other parts of the country who had come to find safety and a roof over their heads, the faces of the people that in their unguarded moments carried a haunted look.

I plunged into an orgy of buying, and decided to make this the year to beat all years in terms of lunches and dinners and outings. I bought everything I could lay my hands on—Pucci, Gucci, Valentino dresses, Cartier bags, Hermes shoes. Nothing was good enough for her ladyship. To think that I was the same woman who had written a book about the civil war that was also against the bourgeois society of 1976.* Here I was as lost as ever: which political faction did I belong to? Must I side with one against the other? Should I be more disgusted by these rather than those? Or should I just be selfish and live without

---

* *Survival in Beirut. A diary of civil war* by Lina Mikdadi Tabbara; Onyx Press, 1979. (Originally published in French as *Survivre dans Beyrouth;* Olivier Orban, 1977.)

looking right, left or centre?

I settled the children at school, got them used to the old routine and scurried off to Paris, partly on business (for the book I had written) but mainly for pleasure. It was November 1977 and a bombshell was about to drop on the Arab world. Unexpected, unbelievable, unimaginable—no word can describe what each Arab nationalist felt when that plane swept down the runway at Lydda Airport and Egypt's President Anwar Sadat stepped out. I sat in a corner at the house of friends in Paris where we were all glued to the television set, still thinking it couldn't be possible, that maybe it was a hoax or a trap.

We and millions of viewers around the world froze as he stood at the top of the stairs with the air of a victorious conqueror, which he was not. Was that the same man of October 1973, the man who took the whole Israeli army by surprise on their Yom Kippur and stunned the world? Or had that too been part of the plot leading up to this very moment when I am lying on my bed and trembling at the sound of the approaching bombers? Part of me is willing my feet to move off the bed and begin the descent to the shelter and part of me is so divorced from reality that I watch myself with a strange mixture of sympathetic interest and detachment.

Tears had run down my cheeks as I watched Sadat meeting our bitter enemies, greeted by Menahem Begin, joking with Moshe Dayan, embracing Golda Meir, and chatting to Abba Eban. One would have thought they were all bosom friends meeting again after a long separation. Anwar Sadat in Jerusalem, a hero to the West, a traitor to the East. In any case, a man with guts, I had reluctantly to admit to myself. Anwar Sadat in Jerusalem—what was going to be the next step? A plan to Balkanise the area? A new Yalta? Another Vietnam? My friends discussed the move heatedly, but all I wanted to do was go out to dinner wishing that Sadat would drop dead by the time we had dessert.

Well Sadat didn't drop dead just then—he went on to Camp David and a peace treaty. Meanwhile, I chose this glorious moment to fall desperately, madly in love with the husband of a friend of mine. Some friend I must have been. Throughout the affair I knew what I was doing was awful, deceitful, dishonest, and yet I could not stop myself although I tried and tried—I probably didn't try hard enough. Was it the civil war that had turned me into a ruthless, selfish human being or had I always been like this, as many people said later when the affair came out into the open?

Things went from bad to worse, in my life and in the country. On March 15th, 1978, Israel invaded Southern Lebanon. I know the Israelis don't need an excuse to attack, but this time they claimed they had one: it was a reprisal for the attack by eleven Fateh guerrillas who landed near Haifa, hijacked a bus to Tel Aviv, and were stopped after a shoot-out with Israel's anti-terrorist squad. The Israelis called the invasion of the South 'Operation Stone of Wisdom'. They said it was a 'limited operation along the Lebanese border to dislodge the terrorist bases from the area' (Ezer Weizman, *The Battle for Peace* p274), but soon extended their operation beyond the original six-mile zone to reach Tyre.

The Lebanese Southerners fled northwards to Beirut by the thousands. Empty apartments, whose owners had gone abroad during the civil war, were quickly occupied by the refugees, and so were buildings still under construction. Armed elements (the usual description of armed men from all shades of the political spectrum) reappeared in the streets, as unshaven as ever. Was it a must, I wondered, never to shave in a revolution? I had the keys to my brother's apartment which I was supposed to be keeping an eye on. I was soon relieved of both the keys and the responsibility by a gentleman with a kalashnikov.

A few days after that invasion I was asked by Jocelyne, a photographer friend of mine, if I would be willing to take her down to the South, to a God-forsaken village below Tyre called Saksakieh. She wanted to go there in search of a family of fifteen, one of whom had escaped to Beirut and kept begging her for information about his family.

'Why not?' I said, 'On condition that you don't tell anyone; people would think we were crazy.' I liked adventure and this was as good as any.

We got into my car at around ten o'clock in the morning and drove south. At first there seemed to be no problem—and no traffic either. We went through busy Sidon like a breeze. As we drove on we started noticing armed elements along the road. They were seated calmly by the roadside, and they didn't interfere with the only car heading south. All the other cars, packed to the brim with people, seemed to be dashing madly in the opposite direction towards Beirut.

Jocelyne and I had the radio on; after all, soft music is soothing to the ear. As we neared the bridge that separated us from Tyre, I decided to drive a bit more carefully. The music was suddenly drowned out by another noise.

'Did you hear that?'

'What?'

'I don't know, there's a strange noise.'

'Slow down your car and turn off the radio,' said Jocelyne.

'My God, it's bombers, planes. . . My God, let's get out of here.' I stopped the car in the middle of the road about fifty metres from the bridge, left the motor running and the radio on, and threw myself into the nearest ditch. The noise the bombers were making was unbelievable, but I couldn't see anything: my face was glued to the ground. All I could think of was how strangely the smell of orange blossoms mixed with gunpowder. It was an eerie feeling. Jocelyne and I seemed to be detached from time; we didn't utter a word, in fact we were barely breathing until it was over.

'The orange blossom,' Jocelyne said jokingly, 'I wish we could pick some.'

'Oh, shut up,' I replied. We got into the car and looked at each other questioningly. I was scared, but did I dare say anything? Oh, no.

'Shall we go on?' she asked.

'Of course.' The bridge had been bombed, but only its sides were damaged. 'Let's go on to Tyre.'

I hadn't visited Tyre in years. When we reached it half an hour later, I could barely recognise the place. We went immediately to the rest house, which had been turned into a headquarters for the International Red Cross. There was only one person there. He was Swiss and, like most Swiss, was calm and unemotional. He directed us to the village we had come to visit and, without further comment, advised us to be careful. At the entrance to the rest house we came across two French journalists who decided to join us—provided we led the way. I looked at Jocelyne and smiled—courage was for women! We got into the car and drove off.

'Ah, here's a sign that directs us to Saksakieh.'

'Watch out,' Jocelyne said softly, 'There seems to be a barricade here.'

I stopped the car, and ten armed elements, speaking almost in unison, told us we had better turn back because the enemy was not far ahead. I looked, saw nothing, and decided to go on—after all, I liked adventure, didn't I? Suddenly I saw the village at the top of a hill; only a turn in the road separated us from it. Jocelyne decided to hang her white scarf out of the window—it was a souvenir from a trip she'd made with the Polisario in the Western Desert.

'What are you doing that for?' I asked.

'Just in case. . .'

'In case of what?'

'Just in case the Israeli army. . .' which was suddenly standing right before us, armed to the hilt. There were Hebrew letters everywhere, and the Star of David here and there. Should I have cried at this encounter with my oldest enemy? Should I have felt scared? The only thing I felt was numbness. I stopped right in my tracks with the Frenchmen behind me and let them do the talking, which they did in English. Orders were fired out, explanations were given, and throughout I sat motionless behind the wheel, looking at the strangers in front of me. These people had taken my father's land in Palestine and turned me into a misfit. They made me what I was today, and yet some of them looked just like me. As a matter of fact, most of them looked more Arab than I did. Had they wanted peace, they wouldn't have stayed in the West Bank and Gaza, in the Golan Heights and parts of Sinai. Had they wanted peace, they wouldn't be here at all, not in Lebanon, not in Syria, not in Jordan.

And when we were ordered to turn back, all I could feel was hatred, frustration and humiliation.

CHAPTER 2

By the summer of 1978, the Israelis had withdrawn and the people of the South had been left to lick their wounds. They didn't know whom to hate more, the Israelis or the Palestinians based in their country. If you tried to explain that the destruction was caused by Israel and not the Palestinians, you might well provoke a blow on the head. Many Southerners had gone home, but some had decided to stay in the apartments they had occupied in Beirut.

Poor Beirut was dirtier than ever, but there were still the plush new Summerland beach resort and the long-established Golf Club as well as the Saint Georges Yacht Club, which stood as a landmark in the desolate hotel district of Beirut that was badly damaged during the civil war. These were the places we frequented to forget the noise and dirt—once inside you could imagine you were in Acapulco. Women paraded in an assortment of bikinis, children ran in the sand, and the men played backgammon and discussed politics while they sipped their drinks. All brands of drink were available—that was about the only thing that never went out of business.

We still plied between West and East Beirut, and telephones had started working again more or less efficiently. Disco had caught on and young and old alike danced to Saturday Night Fever and other hit songs. We swapped gossip and tried to live as if nothing had happened.

Soon we had to put all that aside, though: part of Lebanon was in turmoil again. The wheels of fate had turned and the Phalangists' number one enemy had become the Syrians. Ashrafiye, the eastern part of Beirut, was coming under heavy Syrian artillery fire. We anxiously called our friends and urged them to come and stay with us where it was safe, but most of them preferred to stay put or escape to the mountain resorts. Shelters were prepared in a hurry, others had already been set up; indeed there was talk around town of luxurious shelters equipped with generators, video sets and refrigerators.

Each night I stood on the balcony and watched the scene on the other side; I was really confused. What the hell was happening anyway? The Syrians had originally helped the Phalangists (the Lebanese Christian right-wing movement) take over the Palestinian refugee camp of Tal al-Zaatar; they had helped the Phalangists against the Palestinians and the Lebanese National Movement (a grouping of Lebanese leftist and Muslim organisations) in the last days of the civil war.

Was I supposed to side with anyone or could I simply remain neutral? Some of my best friends were there, helpless under the shelling. And yet I couldn't forget Black Saturday in December 1975 when 365 Muslims were chosen at random and murdered by the Phalangists just because they were Muslims and because four Phalangists had been found assassinated earlier that

12

morning. The Syrians had hit us and so had the Phalangists, but I couldn't help being angry at what was happening in East Beirut. Lebanese citizens were being bombed, not Phalangists. It is always the innocent who pay, rarely the leaders or the people responsible.

Things calmed down. The Syrians withdrew from the Christian side and settled in our areas, and we rarely returned to East Beirut except on visits of condolence. By the end of that summer not only had Ashrafiye been blown apart, but my personal life as well. My famous affair had become even more famous and was now public. I asked for a divorce, got it and went to live in my father's apartment; my father was away at that time and was stunned when he found out what I had done. Shock waves went through our circle of friends—the friends who had known all along. Things were no longer the same now that it was out in the open; people made accusations and counter-accusations and talked endlessly about it. Everyone pretended it was news to them.

I featured as the 'baddy', of course, while all other parties remained blameless. I went from anguish to the depths of despair, with loneliness and self-pity as my only companions. The nights were the worst, and one night I finally gave in to all these feelings. I took a bottle of cointreau, poured out a glass and collected all the bottles of valium I could lay my hands on. I drank a toast to the injustice of the world, only to wake up in hospital the next morning with a dreadful pain in my throat, a headache and a bottle of plasma dangling over my head.

When I asked to leave the hospital, I was told I could only be released when I had seen the police or a psychiatrist. The latter seemed a better choice. The doctor came to my room and asked why I had done the unmentionable (in the orient two things are unmentionable: a suicide attempt or a nervous break-down). 'Well, doctor,' I replied, 'What would you have done if you woke up one day and found yourself all alone with all the doors and windows shut?' That seemed to be reason enough for him, and an hour later I was out, vowing never to do such a stupid thing again. I found out later that my blood pressure had been zero when I reached the hospital and that I had been taken down seven flights on a ladder by friends: there had been no electricity. So I had friends after all! And life wasn't so bad if you had enough patience and guts.

I needed both in the days that followed. People I had considered friends crossed the street to avoid saying hello. It is hard to be a divorcee in the orient, and even harder to be one without a lot of money stashed away. By summer I had had enough of the hypocrisy of the city so I took off to London with my children. I hoped that for a while I could be more than somebody's daughter, wife, sister or mistress. Maybe I could be me. . .

My three brothers lived in England and we visited them all that summer: one was now happily married to his American girlfriend, with a lovely daughter named Ridha after my mother; the second was married to an English girl who was quiet, lovely and always helpful; and the third was on the way to a second marriage, switching from an Iranian to a Scotswoman. My father was well into his second marriage—to a Swiss woman. What a family! The United Nations couldn't have done better, especially as one of the women had a Zionist Jew for a father. But democracy was the name of the game, so no one had ever uttered a word of criticism, mostly because we liked his daughter very much.

At the end of September I went back to Beirut, settled the children in school and moved out of my father's house to a furnished flat, much to his dismay. My life settled into a routine: during the day I took care of the children, whose father had custody, and in the evenings I was alone most of the time. I refused to go out, and spent most of my time reading. New Year's Eve, 1978, I spent alone sobbing my heart out at the noise of revelry outside; 1979 was not much better.

Early in 1980 I took the children on a long-promised trip to the United States, where they were to go to camp in Vermont. We passed through New York, a city I have always loved, but Leyla hated it and Rasha only said she loved it to console me. Neither of them could see in it what I saw: the culture, the lovely museums, the park, the rush to work, the competitive feeling, the gratification when you produced more than others, the variety of fields one could excel in. All they wanted was amusement parks, horses and swings and the company of children their age. I took them to the United Nations, which didn't impress them in the least. In vain did I try to describe how Yasser Arafat had stood proudly at the General Assembly podium in 1974, in vain did I try to tell them about the goals of the United Nations. All they wanted was Vermont and Camp Kiniya. So I left them there and rushed back to Beirut where Marwan, the man I loved, awaited me.

An incident late in 1980 stands out in my mind. I had gone with Marwan (who was still more or less married) to dinner at a small place called Smuggler's Inn. It was the Muslim feast of Al-Adha (the feast of sacrifice) and the place was full of people who had come back from the Gulf to celebrate in Beirut. We sat with a couple of his friends, eating fish, drinking wine and exchanging jokes. One friend had a pistol in his belt.

'What's that for?' we asked.

'To defend you and myself.'

'Oh good, that's a relief. You can never tell what might happen.' Suddenly, several armed men pushed open the door and swarmed in. We all froze—was it a robbery? A kidnapping? We found out soon enough it was armed robbery. All the diners were pushed roughly towards the back where we were seated. It was a very small area and could barely hold 24 people. It suddenly held 40, some standing and some still frozen in their seats.

'Hands up, you mother-fuckers,' one of them ordered.

'And to think you're drinking on a Muslim feast,' said another. The robbers spoke with a strong Palestinian accent, but I knew they were not Palestinian because they were using terms I've never heard the Palestinians use. A woman next to me sobbed in despair. 'Shut up!' I told her encouragingly, 'You should be ashamed of yourself; and watch out for my wine, you're about to spill it on me.' She did, and I calmly wiped the table. The robbers were busy snatching everything away when I remembered my rings. I slipped them quietly off my fingers and dropped them into the pocket of my jeans. I'd long since gone back to jeans—no more Pucci, Gucci, Hermes, Cartier or Valentino for the likes of me!

Suddenly there was an outburst of firing—it seemed Al Capone lived and he was shooting at the floor with an M16 and a kalashnikov. The faces around me went absolutely white; the robbers seemed in a hurry. Marwan, who had remained as calm as I had, took off his watch and dropped it on the floor. When they asked him for it he told them they already had it. Necklaces were wrenched from around the women's throats;

money was snatched from the men, and guns and pistols were collected without ceremony, our friend's included. The look on his face made me want to burst out laughing, but then I thought better of it. Al Capone and his partners disappeared as suddenly as they had arrived. Some women fainted, dropping to the floor like flies, while others fell sobbing into their partners' arms. One man was slightly wounded.

'Let's get out of here,' said Marwan.

'But we haven't paid the bill,' I protested.

He gave me a funny look: 'Sometimes you are stupid—what are we supposed to pay the bill with?'

The next day Marwan told me our things had been found and to go and collect them from one of the armed elements' headquarters. The daring seven had been caught very quickly for a change and had been brought to justice. I asked why he couldn't go himself and was told he was waiting for an important phone call. I picked up the stolen things, which included the watch I had reluctantly relinquished in case they had wondered why a woman wasn't wearing any jewellery. When I got back I found out about that mysterious phone call; Marwan had been appointed Minister of Tourism in the new Lebanese cabinet.

Being a minister in the Lebanon of 1980, I thought, was like being the last minister before Judgement Day. I had a premonition the cabinet would be around a long time, but I was told to shut up as I knew nothing of politics. Strange how men love power. A former Lebanese prime minister is reported to have said once that it was better to ride for ten minutes in a car with number '3' on the licence plate and a pennant flying than to live as an ordinary man for the rest of your life. Well, ministries and premierships didn't impress me in a country like this; I preferred Marwan as a journalist and an excellent one at that. But he too was a man and nothing was going to stand in the way of his ambition.

The winter of 1981 was, for me, a winter of discontent. I still had no work, still spent my days taking care of the children and still went home at night to read. In all this turmoil I discovered a true friend in my stepmother: a wonderful person who never interfered and never sat in judgement. We had a glass of wine together every evening, chatted for a while, and then I went back to my reading and she to her knitting.

In March 1981, Zahle, a town in the mountainous east of

Lebanon that was controlled by Phalangists, found itself facing the fate of Ashrafiye the year before, and suffered heavy Syrian shelling. This time it was more serious: we were told that the Phalangists were trying to cut a road through to Israel, that Syria was trying to stop them, that the number killed was in the hundreds, that the Phalangists had done this, that the Syrians had done that, until finally we poor stupid Lebanese didn't know what to think anymore.

By April 2nd, 1981, the turmoil had reached Beirut; schools closed and panic settled in again. I remember one day, when I was watching a video film, a young cousin came to borrow a few cassettes.

'Hi Nadim, pick up anything you want. I was just about to come and have coffee with your mother. Is she sleeping?'

'No, she's gone to see the family of her cousin who died.'

Her cousin had been assassinated in Tyre a couple of weeks earlier.

'She's gone to visit them again?' I asked.

'No, not that cousin, your cousin,' he explained.

'Which one?'

'Nadia, you know. . . Nadia.' Poor Nadim was becoming flustered.

'Which Nadia?'

'Nadia Kronfol, she was shot by mistake at a Palestinian barricade yesterday night.' She was a cousin on my Lebanese mother's side of the family. I was out of the house before Nadim had finished speaking; he stared after me in bewilderment. I was sobbing my heart out. Nadia and I had never been very close, but somehow, somewhere inside me, I felt I had killed her. For the next seven days I didn't know what to do to help my family forget this tragic event and how it had come about. I sent cables of protest to the Palestinian leadership, made phone calls, sat for hours taking part in the condolences. I was both angry and upset; she had so loved life, the poor woman, and had died such a stupid death.

CHAPTER 3

In August 1981 Marwan organised a sort of mini-festival in the Roman ruins of Baalbek where Lebanon's annual arts festival used to be held. To reach Baalbek you have to pass through Zahle, where all was quiet once more. Life had gone back to normal after all the bombing and shelling, and the Lebanese, with their usual vitality and love of life, had begun to rebuild whatever had been destroyed. The Syrian army was posted outside the town, the Lebanese army inside. The town itself was all hustle and bustle again and the traffic jams delayed us.

Baalbek was as majestic as ever, its columns rising up to the sky, its temples still erect and waiting for their respective gods. The gods may not have put in a physical appearance but we mortals certainly felt their presence when we entered the ruins and heard once more the long-lost music of the Baalbek Festival. Some of the women discreetly wiped away a tear; I felt goose-pimples all over my body at the sight of such forgotten magnificence. As we sat on the stones in the amphitheatre and waited for the show to begin, I closed my eyes and remembered how I had come to Baalbek in 1957 when the festival was first opened. I could see the well-known Lebanese singer Fairouz on the stage, hear Hamlet and Ophelia speak, watch Nureyev and Margot Fonteyn dance. I remembered the joyful rush to Baalbek every summer after that, all the lovely women there, all the splendour, the grandeur of that festival which had become known the world over.

Tonight, only the ordinary Lebanese were there, trying to recapture a little of the past, however small. The Lebanese folklore troupe Caracalla, which has performed in Europe and America, was here in force. They had arranged everything: dinner among the ruins in a lovely oriental tent, the music, the bedouin dancing. Even their special star, the former beauty queen Marcelle, had come out of the hospital for the weekend to have one last look at the Baalbek she loved most. She was twenty-seven years old and she was dying of cancer. Everybody knew it and no one held out any hope, but she hoped as she struggled on and never complained. She could barely walk and she certainly couldn't eat, only sip a little of her medicine. Yet here she was, all smiles and as beautifully dressed as ever, although she was painfully thin and white as a sheet.

It was a wonderful evening as Baalbek worked its magic— but nothing could bring back the past. We were only fooling ourselves. It was with a sense of deep loss that I left the city the next day. I wondered if I would ever see it again.

On the way back we decided to go in search of the famous Syrian Soviet-made Sam missiles that had created such a great to-do in Israel. We thought we could see ramps on either side of the road that led to Damascus, but we never saw a trace of the missiles. What we did see was hashish growing everywhere—there no longer seemed to be any need for the sunflowers that had previously been grown to hide that thriving plant. In Baalbek you could have your hash in your tea, in your *tabbouleh* (a famous Lebanese salad), on your hubbly-bubbly, in water, on the rocks, whichever way you wanted it, even in your kebab. A great industry, hash: roads have been built for it, cut through the rocky mountains, people have been killed for it, others have grown rich on it. Hash, one of the slow roads to dementia and death—you could smell it everywhere.

Marcelle died on a wintry Tuesday morning without ever losing consciousness. I had seen her the day before and all I could think was: I hope she dies soon.

For the first time in four years I set foot in East Beirut, where her funeral procession was to be held. I didn't take my car but went by taxi, asking the driver to wait for me as long as was necessary. Nothing was going to stop me from bidding farewell to Marcelle and her youth. The place where she lay was covered with rose petals. She was young and unmarried so her funeral was to be her wedding: that is our tradition. Her brother and sister went around offering soft drinks and pastries; her colleagues got up in unison at one point to perform a farewell dance around the open coffin. Finally, they put the lid on amidst the screams and wailing of the women.

We went down to the street; her family had decided to walk all the way to church. As we walked slowly down the streets of the East Beirut suburb of Ain al-Rummaneh (where all our misery began on April 13th, 1975, when the spark was struck that launched the civil war in earnest), I heard shop shutters close in respect. I saw women make the sign of the cross, men stop their cars and get out, children throw rice and rose petals from their balconies on to the procession below. I saw that all the Lebanese were still the same in the face of death, respectful when it was individual, indifferent when it was collective.

I also noticed, in spite of myself, that the streets were cleaner here than in West Beirut (fascist law and order, I was told when

I went back West) and that there were no armed elements in sight throughout our fifty-minute walk. Yet I still preferred my way of life in my side of the city.

Marcelle's final resting place was in Baalbek facing the ruins of the Temple of Bacchus. She was met by all the people she loved so much at the entrance to the city: Christians and Muslims alike came out to salute her courage and fortitude and to give her the farewell she deserved.

Today she's alive and with the gods: we're the dead.

CHAPTER 4

I finally found a home of my own—well, it wasn't really my own it was my cousin's, but she had lent it to me lock, stock and barrel for a year. At first I called it Ghada's apartment, but in a few weeks I got so used to it I would say, 'I'm going home,' and that was a comforting feeling. A place of my own with no one to nag or interfere after the years of moving around from my father's house to furnished apartments to friends' houses.

Marwan and I went out from time to time, but we preferred to spend most evenings at home playing canasta, a card game that brings out the worst in people. Each time we played canasta the house shook with shouting and swearing, and I swore I would never play it again—until the next evening. Another great pastime was having our fortunes read in coffee cups. A friend of ours, Mouna, was a great cup-reader, and we laughingly consulted her every day. In November she told me that next year would bring me great hardship and misery, that I would be stretched taut as an elastic band. I decided she was not such a great cup-reader after all. I hadn't had a very easy time lately—surely things couldn't become any more difficult?

In the winter of that year the whole country seemed to be slipping, more than ever before. Suicide attempts, nervous breakdowns and divorces had become the order of the day. You could hardly say hello to anyone any more without having your head snapped off. Had the civil war made us like that—impatient, irritable and intolerant—and were the cracks at last beginning to show? The high rate of divorce was not difficult to explain: you can put up with a lot in an ordered system, particularly since divorce is considered shameful in an oriental society.

Once all hell broke loose and society itself disintegrate̶
no one cared any more what people thought of one ano̶

One of my brothers in England received his bombshell ̶
December. His American wife upped and left one night, taking
their three- and five-year-old daughters with her. She was in love
with his best friend—who was also his cousin by marriage and
his boss. At one blow my brother had lost everything: wife,
children, home and job.

Two days later my eldest brother's second wife died in a fall
from the fifth floor of their house. Was it an accident or suicide?
I didn't want to know. She was 29 years old and left behind her
a 13-year-old girl and an 11-month-old baby. It was awful.
There was nothing I could do from where I was in Beirut but
watch the shambles my family was becoming, and try to pick
up the pieces. After a few weeks of absolute misery, I went into
my cocoon again, wanting never to emerge. I saw the friends
I had left, and read and read, collecting all the books I could lay
my hands on. What was happening in my family seemed to be a
microcosm of the world around us, but when I tried to explain
this to people around me they told me not to worry, that things
were getting better in Lebanon, that time was the great healer.

In the end it was easier to believe what people said, that
things were getting better, that they were fine. Leyla, who
hadn't been doing too well at the beginning of the year, had
become quite a good student by spring 1982, thanks to her
determination and a bit of help from me. I had been apartment
hunting and was nearing success, although trying to find an
apartment in Beirut in those days was murder; prices had sky-
rocketed and one year's rent was what we would have paid to
buy a flat before the civil war. Incomes had not risen to match
prices. My cousin Ghada was coming back on June 28th so I
had to find a place before then. I had tried in vain to persuade
her to postpone her return for another year, but she was
adamant. She missed the Golf Club, her friends, the hustle and
bustle of Beirut, its dirt and its noise. I couldn't understand
why someone who had a fine house on the Potomac would
want to come back to this huge jail called Lebanon.

On Saturday May 29th, I gave a dinner at Ghada's place.
It was a magnificent one, and little did I know then it would
be the 'Last Supper'. We danced, laughed and sang, trying
again to forget the present, recapture the past, and look forward

to the future. A neighbour later said that the odour of hash had reached her doorstep eight flights down. Well, there had been no hash, we were happy enough without it and didn't need it.

On Thursday June 3rd, I sipped my coffee early in the morning and read the newspapers. The Falklands War still captured the headlines. . . Port Stanley was on the verge of falling to the British. If nothing else, Mrs Thatcher certainly acted in times of tension. I wished we had someone to do that in Lebanon, or in the Middle East for that matter, where the situation hadn't improved for the past decade. There were even some new aspects to the imbroglio in the Middle East, like the raging war between Iraq and Iran which was reflected daily on the Lebanese stage with the Shias (a pro-Iranian Muslim sect) and members of the pro-Iraqi Baath Party regularly killing one another. The Iraqi embassy in Beirut had been literally flattened by an explosion in which some sixty-five people had been killed, including the ambassador. Chargés d'affaires from various embassies were being assassinated like something out of a spy story, car bombs exploded here and there killing innocent people. And the saddest incident of all was the assassination of the well-liked and respected French ambassador Louis Delamare. West Beirut had its good days and its bad days, but it remained unstable.

Philip Habib, President Reagan's special envoy to the Middle East, who had negotiated the Israeli-Palestinian ceasefire in July 1981 along Lebanon's border with Israel, was to come back with a package deal. His favourite comment on the situation: 'No comment.' He was said to be proposing more United Nations forces for the so-called 'Free Lebanon' area controlled by renegade Lebanese major Saad Haddad. Haddad was backed in his enclave by the Israelis, who had turned that border area over to him rather than withdrawing from the whole of South Lebanon after their invasion in 1978.

One could always hope for the best, but I felt there was something disturbing in the news. Menahem Begin was talking of Palestinian reinforcements in the South, and the Palestinians were saying the same about the Israelis.

To say the least, 'something is rotten' in the state of Lebanon. I remembered the conclusion I had come to in the book I wrote on the civil war, *Survival in Beirut*. I had added these lines to the English edition in autumn 1978:

22

People are still being kidnapped, never to be found again. Maybe those who left, like my brother Nayer, were right after all. The snowball is still rolling; neither Washington nor Moscow seem to want to stop it. I can see no logic behind the current of events, no matter what the final analysis, only absurdity. But then, I am neither in Washington nor am I in Moscow; I live in the ruins of what used to be the Switzerland of the Middle East. Every event in the world seems to be linked to the Lebanese bloodbath in one way or another: PLO representatives shot down in London, Kuwait, Paris. . . Iraqis hit in London, Paris, Beirut, Islamabad. . . a coup d'état in Afghanistan. . . the war in Ethiopia. . . a bloodless (that term still exists!) coup d'état in Mauritania. . . a Polisario ceasefire. . . Aldo Moro of Italy and the Red Brigades. . . maybe even the Korchnoi-Karpov chessgame in Baguio City. A deadly game, chess, but not as deadly as the game played in Lebanon where two peoples, the Lebanese and the Palestinians, seem to have bought, willingly or otherwise, a one-way ticket to annihilation.

At 11.30 in the evening of Thursday June 3rd, 1982, Israeli Ambassador Shlomo Argov came out of the Dorchester Hotel in London. He had just had dinner with eighty-four other ambassadors. Two young men were waiting for him outside the hotel which overlooks Hyde Park, but they were not looking at the park. A few minutes later the Ambassador lay on the ground, with several bullets in his head.

On Friday June 4th at 6.45 in the morning I'd just come home after sending the children off to school. Leyla and Rasha attended the College Louise Wegmann, which was in a peaceful village called Bchemoun beyond the southern outskirts of Beirut. It took them one hour to get there and one hour to come back every day, and they loved every minute of that ride in the school bus, even passing the biggest rubbish dump in the area, which graced a place called Khalde in the southern suburbs of Beirut. They had made a game out of that trip past the rubbish dump; all thirty-four children, the youngest crushed by the eldest, rushed to the windows holding their noses, shut the windows, breathed in again and smelt all the mingled odours of whatever was lying there rotting (which sometimes included dead cows), then laughed their heads off like little maniacs. God only knows what they found so funny. This game was repeated twice every day.

That Friday I wasn't thinking of the children and their games. I was really worried about the news of the assassination attempt the night before. What was going to happen to us? I asked that question of everybody I met that morning. Some didn't answer, some laughed at me: 'What has it got to do with us?' they asked.

'What do you mean, what has it got to do with us?' I snapped back, 'First, let me tell you that even if the assassins had come from Katmandu we would still be blamed; second, if that ambassador dies it's a catastrophe.' Let's face it, I added to myself, whether he dies or not, we're in for it. At any rate, there was nothing I could do about it, so I tried to put it out of my mind.

That day I had more important business to attend to. I was at the end of my six-month search for a flat; I had finally found one to let. At last I was going to have a place I could really call my own. I loved it already although it was a quarter of the size of the places I had lived in before. At eleven o'clock that morning I met the owner, cheques and receipts changed hands. We agreed to sign the contract once it had been re-painted, and I sighed with relief. I decided to take two of my friends out to lunch at Chez Jean-Pierre, one of the few remaining restaurants in West Beirut and my favourite place. Only the brave and the crazy went to Jean-Pierre's: it was on the top floor of a very old building right in the ruined centre of the city. Half the time there was no electricity, so you had to tramp up the four flights of stairs, after pushing through a crowd of curious, wide-eyed ragamuffin children at the entrance. The owners were even stranger than the surroundings. They were French-Algerians who considered themselves more Lebanese than the Lebanese, and they nagged about everything: the electricity, the water supply, the telephone that never worked, the refuse collectors and the rubbish heap by the seaside which had been turned into a natural barricade by the Syrians. The more the owner liked you, the more he nagged; yet he was a wonderful old man with a good heart, full of memories, and a whiz at name-dropping. His was the best French food to be had in West Beirut; when Beirut was at its peak you had to book a table days in advance.

I walked in with my two friends Amal and Ismat to find two of the tables occupied by foreign correspondents—that was already very busy by Jean-Pierre's post-war standards. We chose to sit on the balcony that had a magnificent view of the Saint Georges bay. There were a lot of water-skiers, speedboats and fishermen casting their lines from the rocks; it was a beautiful day and the food was, as usual, delicious. We drank a toast to my new flat and discussed various ways to decorate it; I was going to turn it into a house-owner's dream on a few hundred pounds!

It was five past three in the afternoon—time for a cointreau. It was a wonder I hadn't become an alcoholic after 1975; before then I'd hardly touched drink. Now I drank a lot, smoked even more and ate far less. I was constantly warned that I'd end up in an asylum, in Alcoholics Anonymous or dying of lung cancer; it always struck me as funny that no one mentioned a bullet or a bomb as the possible cause of an early trip to the hereafter.

At nine minutes past three, I sipped my cointreau and kept an eye on my watch; I would have to leave in fifteen minutes to meet Leyla and Rasha at their home: they returned at exactly 3.45 every afternoon. We suddenly heard a faint noise above, and several white lines criss-crossed the sky.

'What's that?'

'Oh nothing, just Israeli planes,' one of my friends replied.

'What do you mean, nothing? We've had two air raids in the last twelve months and quite murderous ones at that.'

'Oh shut up, they're only taking a few photographs like they usually do,' said one.

'They want a souvenir,' joked another.

Suddenly the journalists inside got very excited, rushed out on to the balcony with their cameras in hand, and started taking pictures.

'Oh my God, look, they're dropping bombs.'

'Where, where?'

'Over there, right in front of you! Jesus Christ, the smoke.'

'Let's go and have a closer look.'

'Let's get out of here!'

'My children, I have to go to my children.'

'Oh shut up, there's nothing wrong with your children.'

'Shut up yourself, you don't even know where they're

bombing.' The time for joking and gossip was over; the cointreau sat untouched; fear, rudeness and a kind of excitement prevailed.

The Israeli bombers seemed to be hitting anything in sight south of Beirut, and parts of the capital itself. Could they recognise a school bus from up there, I wondered frantically. Israeli supremacy in the air was renowned, especially among the Lebanese; we were told that an Israeli pilot could spot a pin from his cockpit. Oh God, I thought, my children and their thirty-two small friends are goners.

'I'll pay you later, I'd better go, Amal, Ismat, I'll see you tomorrow.' I rushed to the children's home, parked the car and looked out. Everybody was out on the streets looking up. That was the way it was in Lebanon; we were all spectators, interested but blasé so long as the 'incident' didn't come too close; we were fearless, yet fearful.

'Have the children arrived yet?' I asked their concierge.

'No.'

I tried to remain calm in front of the spectators, but not for long. Ten minutes later I took off again, heading towards Khalde, crying like a baby, my imagination running ahead of me, seeing my children dead, the school bus burned out. . . I didn't get very far.

'Where do you think you're going?' the Syrian soldier asked at the barricade near the UNESCO building at Beirut's southern exit.

'To Bchemoun.'

'Are you crazy? The Israelis are bombing Bchemoun.'

I nearly fainted from anguish. I turned back to the north and sped towards the house of a friend of mine, Leyla Khalaf, who was one of the College's administrators. She also had two children on the school bus and if anyone knew anything she would. Leyla was very white in the face, but calm and encouraging; her mother and aunt were in tears, and I quickly joined in. I was told the children had left school at five past three—some reassurance.

'Where are they bombing?'

'We don't know.'

'Could they have gone back to the school?'

'No, we just managed to get through to the headmistress, she's standing vigil but no school bus has returned.'

I tried to pull myself together, went to the children's house and had a cointreau. That did the trick. I went and stood on the balcony, like hundreds of parents who were waiting for their children to come home from school. There was nothing to say: the horror of what we saw before us was beyond imagining. There was smoke everywhere in the direction of the South, the sound of the explosions, the ear-splitting noise as the bombers broke through the sound barriers.

The children got home two hours later. The bus driver looked as if he was in a state of shock. Leyla and Rasha were quite excited.

'Mummy, there was a bit of shooting on the way, that's why we're late. The school bus hid in a hole. I hope you weren't worried. Have you been crying?'

'No.'

'Are you sure? Good. Let's go, we have to study for next week's exams.'

I looked at them in wonder: hadn't they realised the danger they'd been through? All that concerned my daughters was to get ready for their final exams early so that they could attend their cousin Randa's wedding on June 10th. They talked of nothing else. I wondered if they were suppressing their feelings or if they were simply fearless; I made a mental note to ask a psychiatrist. What Leyla and Rasha didn't know was that the air raids had killed 60 people and wounded 270, not to mention the destruction and the surge of refugees from the bombed areas to central Beirut.

Politically, the results were even more complicated. Lebanon requested a UN Security Council meeting; the French Foreign Minister Claude Cheysson declared that the European Foreign Ministers, meeting at Versailles, were 'flabbergasted'; American Secretary of State Alexander Haig linked the Israeli air raids to the assassination attempt in London, as if he were trying to justify them. The American State Department refused to indicate whether it considered the raids a violation of the July 1981 ceasefire. A statement noted that the US Government was 'profoundly preoccupied' by the 'new acts of violence that have been carried out in Lebanon in answer to the despicable assassination attempt on the Israeli Ambassador in London, Mr Shlomo Argov.'

Thousands of miles away in New Delhi, the Kuwaiti First

Secretary had been assassinated by two young men. Should we therefore anticipate a 'Kuwaiti retaliation' in Lebanon? Why not, since everything that happens abroad seems to turn back on us?

CHAPTER 5

Shlomo Argov lay fighting for his life in a London hospital, while the death toll rose slowly in Lebanon. It was rather hard to fight for one's life here; against aerial bombardment, either you made it or you didn't.

It was Saturday June 5th, that day when exactly fifteen years ago the Six-Day War broke out, ending in tragedy for the Arabs and success for the Israelis. At 1.15 in the morning in June 1982, Israel launched a large-scale operation in South Lebanon. It began with a sixteen-hour battle during which all areas south of Beirut down to the border were bombed: not one was missed. The bombardment came by air, sea and land; they hadn't yet found a way to bomb underground as well. The toll in human lives? 150 dead, 250 wounded.

Israeli Prime Minister Menahem Begin called it 'Operation Peace for Galilee', vowing that no Palestinian fighter would henceforth be able to fire katyousha rockets at Galilee. I hadn't realised it was possible to reach Galilee from Doha and Bchemoun, two residential areas just outside Beirut. I would have called it 'Operation Bloodbath'—Menahem Begin was no dove.

I found the best definition of the difference between hawks and doves in the book I had begun reading by Ezer Weizman, Israel's former Minister of Defence. He had written in his *Battle for Peace:*

> In peace, no less than in war—we must be prepared to take risks. I have yet to meet the commander who can predict the outcome of an engagement. A good general is not one who launches a plan and then sits back and waits but one who can rectify foul-ups and, equally, leap at unforeseen opportunities.
>
> That is why hawks made good commanders. . . [people] do not understand what a hawk really is. A dove bills and

coos, fluttering in hesitation and uncertainty, while a hawk swoops down, seizes the initiative, and takes advantage of changing situations to serve his cause.

Doves and hawks are like different types of airplanes. A dove is a slow machine, a hawk a fast one. A slow-flying plane has no choice: it flies at low speeds because it lacks the ability to go any faster. But a hawk has the choice: it can fly at top speed or slow down. With its greater flexibility, it is the hawk that can maneuver better in an unknown situation. [p389]

Well, Menahem Begin was definitely a hawk, a blind hawk who flew at top speed whenever he could and seized all the prey that came within range. In this case, most of his prey were innocent civilians who couldn't tell the difference between a katyousha and an RPG (rocket-propelled grenade).

The moment of truth had finally arrived—but what was the use, I wondered in resignation? How could one possibly fight Israeli air supremacy? Thirty-eight towns and villages had been shelled during those sixteen hours, first from the air, then the artillery stepped in. The Israelis were fascinating in their command of technological warfare; they were good at hitting from a distance because they couldn't afford a high death toll which the generals would have to justify to the people. We, on the other hand, seemed to have the importance of flies in their eyes; I wondered if their pilots felt anything when they dropped their bombs, or were they devoid of feeling?

I wished I were James Joyce to be able to express without thinking all that was suppressed inside me. Who had done this to us originally? I mean to all of us? Was it Adam and Eve? Louis XVI? Stalin? That crazed Hitler? Johnson? Khruschev? We always seemed to find someone else to blame for our miseries, both private and public. Why didn't we start with ourselves? Why had my father left Palestine in 1948? That was the year when, at the age of six, I broke that watermelon; I still remembered as clearly as if it had happened yesterday. My father had a piece of land somewhere near Tulkarm (on the West Bank, the West Bank now occupied by all those Israeli settlements). Whose fault was it, that broken watermelon? Who was causing all the misery and suffering? I couldn't stand it any longer, the heartache and the hardship; nor could the Lebanese,

29

or the Palestinians, or, for that matter, the Israelis. It was time to put a stop to all this bloodshed, time for a just and durable peace. . .

But not on June 5th, 1982, that was not the day for peace; it was the time for war, all-out war, for death not for life or hope, for revenge a thousand times over. . .

'Please, can we go over the French dictation?'

That was my daughter Rasha, who brought me out of my daydreaming with amazing suddenness. She was worried about her end-of-year exams and about her cousin's wedding; her white party dress and golden sandals were already in her closet.

'Will we be able to go to Randa's wedding?' she asked.

'Of course you will.'

'What about the bombing?'

'Oh, that should be over by then. We're still five days away from the wedding.'

'But I saw pictures of the highway. We can't get there by car. The Israelis have ruined the road.'

'No they haven't,' I replied reassuringly, 'Don't worry, you'll certainly make it to the wedding.'

'Okay, now can we go over my lessons.' The last thing I felt like doing was reciting verbs over and over again; I was busy getting drunk with a vodka-orange, trying to forget that I was getting drunk—wasn't that what the Little Prince was told by his alcoholic friend?

'What are those planes flying over us?' Rasha asked as she laid out her books on the living-room floor.

'They're Israeli planes.'

'What are they doing?'

'They're bombing the south of Lebanon.'

'Oh. Where is the south of Lebanon?'

'From Khalde on, you know, where the rubbish dump is.'

'Who are they bombing?'

'Everybody who lives there,' I exclaimed, then wondered if I was being objective enough when I said that. After all, the Israelis claimed they were only after military targets—Palestinian military targets, that is—but what about all the innocents who paid with their lives for these targets?

'Don't we have planes to fight their planes?' Rasha persisted.

'No we don't.' As a matter of fact Lebanon does not have fighter planes.

30

'Why not?'

'We can't afford to buy them.'

'And Israel can?'

'Sometimes yes and sometimes no, but the United States helps them a lot.'

'Who helps us?'

'I don't know, maybe the Arab countries will. . .'

'Well, I'm not going to help anybody when I grow up,' Rasha announced.

I kept quiet and hoped she would forget this statement by the time she grew up—if she got the chance to grow up. I shuddered at the thought and touched wood; small traditions were deeply encrusted in me and touching wood to protect us from evil had become a daily habit by then. The planes had not stopped their ballet-like performance over Beirut; in the midst of all this the doorbell rang six times. I recognised the ring as my father's famous way of announcing himself. But that was impossible: he was supposed to be in Switzerland. I opened the door and there he stood.

'What, may I ask, are you doing here?' I said.

'I'm coming to pay the children a visit,' he replied calmly.

'In these conditions?'

'What conditions?' he said. 'Everything is fine.'

My father was something else; he had had so many problems in his life that lately he seemed to have decided to live in a world of his own. He read no newspapers, heard no radios and never watched television. He told me he had been stranded at Larnaca while waiting for Beirut Airport to reopen which in the end it did, and he added reassuringly that everything was fine.

My father, like most of world opinion, did not think that what was happening was a very important matter; it was only a limited operation. I thought of what Ezer Weizman had written about limited operations being better than large ones so as not to arouse world indignation. Weizman had described the Israeli invasion of Lebanon in March 1978, when he was Defence Minister, like this:

It was not the first time that concern for the safety of innocent civilians had restricted the dimensions of our cross-border operations. Our sorties into Lebanon almost always

31

ran into great difficulties on this score. The terrorists mingled with the civilian population, which sheltered their activities—at times, the terrorist positions were no more than a few paces from a hospital or school, a church or mosque.

At first, I was not as concerned about harming the Lebanese population, in view of its cooperation with its terrorists. If civilians were hurt—even unintentionally—I hoped that would goad the Lebanese into casting the PLO groups out from their midst. I had in mind the example of the Jordanian border in the late 1960s: when terrorist incursions from east of the Jordan River had multiplied, our bombs and shells had reduced the Jordan Valley—formerly a veritable paradise—into a desolate wilderness. Tens of thousands of villagers had fled to Amman, ultimately forcing King Hussein to take action against the terrorists. He did so effectively: no Israeli has ever killed terrorists in numbers to rival those felled by the Jordanian King. That showdown occurred in September 1970—the month named 'Black September'. . .

Though directed against the terrorists, our massive actions in Lebanon—shellings and aerial bombings—aroused world opinion against us. Foreign television commentators, who never showed much interest in thousands of children dying of starvation in Cambodia, drew tears from the eyes of millions of viewers by filming a Palestinian child grubbing in the rubble of his home. Accusing Israel of 'a massacre of the Palestinians', they linked those operations with the peace negotiations, alleging that the reprisals were an attempt to annihilate the Palestinian people and deny it the self-determination it was fighting for. [pp 267-268]

I tried to explain to my father that this did not look like a small-scale, limited operation, but an all-out invasion of Lebanon.

'Have you been eating properly?' my father asked.

I decided never to discuss politics with him again; he was much better off where he was, in his own world. There was no point telling him that the UN Security Council had ordered a ceasefire—he would only laugh cynically; there was no point in informing him that the Europeans were very concerned—he would only smile ironically; and what was the use of explaining

32

what Baabda (the seat of the Presidency in Lebanon) saw as its main objective—saving the Habib mission.

That Saturday, June 5th, Yasser Arafat was in Riyadh (Saudi Arabia), Walid Joumblatt (the Druze leader of the Lebanese National Movement) was in Paris, the Lebanese Minister of Information Michel Eddé was on his way back from Moscow. Everybody else was here and quite worried: Israel should withdraw immediately and unconditionally. We were really in a position to issue orders! From what I could see we were getting a hell of a beating, and I felt desolate. What was going to happen to us?

On June 6th, 1967, all the Arab fighter planes lay burning on the ground. We had lost that war, that long-awaited, long-prepared-for war. On Sunday June 6th, 1982, the Israelis invaded the South on three fronts. In Beirut we heard about the street battles in Nabatieh, an attack on Sidon, fierce Syrian-Israeli battles in the region of Hasbaya, Tyre was under siege and resisting as was Beaufort Castle (the old Crusader castle in the South). The Lebanese cabinet was constantly in session (for a change).

On the local level, the Maronite Patriarch called for 'a deep attachment to the dignity of all of Lebanon', the Mufti (the Sunni Muslim religious leader) 'deplored the indifference of both Western and Arab nations', the Shia religious leader expressed surprise at the 'Arab silence'. The most disturbing news that day was the report that the US Embassy had reduced its staff by half.

One piece of good news was the capture of an Israeli pilot. That was truly an achievement: fighter planes shot down by kalashnikovs or RPGs. Israeli pilot Ahiaz Aharon was not exactly well-received by the villagers when he dropped out of the sky—but I didn't think Palestinian prisoners were much better treated by the Israelis when they were captured.

I woke up at five o'clock in the morning on Tuesday June 8th, although there was no need for me to go to the children's house to get them ready for school since there was no school. I just couldn't sleep; things seemed to have worsened at the military level. The leaders who were away had returned: Arafat was back in Beirut and Joumblatt had gone back by way of Damascus to Mukhtara, his fiefdom in the Chouf. Nobody expected any harm or danger to reach the Chouf because there were no fedayeen there. There was plenty of danger in other areas though, all the way along the seafront from the border to Doha, a residential area just south of Beirut. Israel's invasion already covered three times the territory it had occupied in March 1978. Well, people around me said, if the worst comes to the worst we can always sneak away to safety in the Chouf, that impregnable Druze stronghold.

Meanwhile Sidon was under assault from all sides—the people of Southern Lebanon's largest city didn't know what had hit them. Tyre had already fallen. I was in despair at the news: this wasn't a war, this was a massacre. It looked like it was high time to pack up and leave for the Chouf, but I had no intention of going anywhere; I was fine where I was.

'Have you heard the latest?' a friend exclaimed.

'What, what's the latest?' I asked, dreading to hear the answer because his face was so pale.

'They've gone into the Chouf.'

'Who, the Syrians?'

'No, the Israelis,' he answered.

'That's impossible!'

'It's just been announced on Radio Lebanon.'

'It's impossible. The Chouf has four lines of defence, all the way up to Niha. And anyway, what do they want with the area, there are no Palestinians there.'

'How the hell would I know? I'm not an Israeli.'

It was difficult talking to anybody those days; some people's faces were pale and drawn, others red with excitement. Within a few hours all of the Chouf had fallen to the Israelis—Deir al-Qamar, Beiteddine, Baaqline, Ain Zhalta and Mukhtara—without one shot being fired and without one iota of resistance. I was stunned: what had happened to all the armed elements, all the militarily trained people who had paraded in formation every other Sunday for years? What about the guns, the cannons? Where were they when the Israelis walked into the Chouf? Perhaps they were waiting to conduct commando raids against the occupying forces, as these were more suited to the light weapons they carried.

The Israeli occupation of the Chouf had given them an easy entrance to the rest of Lebanon. On Tuesday evening, this was where we stood: heavy Syrian-Israeli battles on the Beirut-Damascus highway, so that road was closed; Tyre had fallen in spite of heavy resistance acknowledged even by the enemy; so had Beaufort Castle, which spelled disaster for whoever was pro-Palestinian as that was the most important Palestinian stronghold in the South; Sidon was under assault from all sides; some reports said the Israelis had reached Saadiyat, which was barely thirty-five minutes from Beirut by car.

Rasha was still worried about her exams and her cousin's wedding, and so was Leyla. As for my father, it was clear when he came to see the children that afternoon on his regular visit that he thought the Israelis were still in Tel Aviv where they belonged.

'What made you decide to come back to Beirut just now?' I asked.

'I have work to attend to,' he said impatiently. My father was an agricultural engineer, and most of his work involved the agricultural land in the south, mainly around Sidon and Tyre. I wondered if he knew what was happening there but I would understand if he didn't; he'd seen it all before and he'd probably had enough. I decided the best thing would be to try to get him out before the situation got worse.

'Do you want to go back to Switzerland?' I asked.

'Is the airport open?' This was going to be difficult: the last plane to land at the airport was the one he had arrived in. I suggested he should leave by way of Jounieh and Tripoli in Lebanon, to Homs and Damascus in Syria. I found a car that would take him and the next morning it showed up at his apartment at five o'clock in the morning already carrying other passengers to Damascus. 'Where am I going anyway?' my father asked in bewilderment and despair. That day and the next I waited by the telephone in agony; had he made it to Damascus or had a stray bomb hit them on the way? At noon the following day I found out that he had arrived and sighed with relief; now I could go back to the war and its shattering news.

But the really shattering news was that, in all the turmoil, I had forgotten my daughter Leyla's birthday. She had turned eleven on the previous day, and was now sobbing her heart out.

'Leyla, I'll take you to lunch, stop crying. Listen, everything has been closed since yesterday, but do you know what I'll do when the shops reopen? I'll buy you anything you want; for heaven's sake stop crying.' Her sobbing was making me nervous.

'I can't,' she wailed.

'I'm sorry I forgot. I know I shouldn't have, I'm sorry. . .'

'It's not because of my birthday.'

'What is it then?'

'They're going to kill you.'

'Who's going to kill me?'

'They are.'

What was she talking about? I didn't know how much she knew about what was going on, but then I knew that we adults were stupid enough to talk freely before children, so she must have collected bits and pieces. I spoke to her very patiently.

'Who are you talking about?'

'The Israelis. I know they're going to kill you.'

'Why? I don't even have any weapons.'

'Because you're half-Palestinian. You've always told me that.'

'Of course I am, but that doesn't mean they're going to kill me, and anyway, I'm Lebanese.'

I tried to explain, to ease her fears, but I didn't know how. The situation was so messy. One had only to open the newspapers to see the messages from the different embassies to their citizens: Ambassade Van Het Koninkrijk der Nederlanden; Die Botschaft der Bundesrepublik Deutschland. I didn't understand a word, but I got the message: get out while you still can!

The military situation was pretty messy too: fierce fighting now in the upper parts of the Chouf, in the western part of the Bekaa, at Khalde (the southern entrance to Beirut's suburbs). The rest seemed already to have been occupied, including Doha where poor Randa's wedding was to have been held.

'Let's play monopoly, Leyla, just you and I.'

That prompted Leyla's first smile that day. Monopoly meant a three-hour game and she loved it. At lunchtime I took Leyla, Rasha and Miriam—one of the few remaining little girls they knew—to the Bristol Hotel.

'Oh, that's great,' Rasha said, 'At least the restaurant is underground.'

'I thought you weren't afraid,' I said.

'Well, not really. . . but it's better.'

'Would you like to work for the Red Cross?' I asked the three little girls. They responded with shouts of enthusiasm. There was now a ceasefire, and I thought that the Red Cross would be as good a place as any for children; maybe the Israelis would remember some parts of the Geneva Convention if they came

36

across them there. In the afternoon, we went and played scrabble at Miriam's. Suddenly, the world seemed to erupt around us; bombers appeared out of nowhere and air raid followed air raid. That couldn't have been a ceasefire they'd reached, but a leasefire!

'It's nothing,' Miriam's mother Irene and I told the children. But, I thought, if that's nothing I'd hate to find out what 'something' might be. I tried in vain to concentrate on a word to place on the board.

'Can't we continue our game another day?' I asked the children.

'Oh, no!' They had believed our reassurances and decided to ignore the nerve-shattering noise. So we continued the game while I tried to appear nonchalant listening to the news on the radio. There were Israeli bombers everywhere, and so far about 207 people were reported killed and 647 wounded. About a hundred people who were fleeing to Syria on the Damascus road had been killed. The worst news that day was the confirmation that Israel had destroyed most of the Sam missiles the Syrians had placed on the Bekaa.

Israel was really at the gates of Beirut; we had no news of anyone in Doha. The only bright spot was that the people of Sidon were still resisting. The city would fall eventually, but with honour, and that was something no patriot could under-estimate. At the refugee camp of Ain al-Helwe on the outskirts of Sidon, thirty people in a bunker refused to give themselves up for days and when they finally did it was because they had run out of ammunition. They inflicted heavy losses on the enemy. The Israeli officer who took the bunker was startled to see thirty children march out, aged between eight and fourteen. He could not help but feel admiration for the thirty boys who had refused to give in because they believed so firmly in their cause—the Palestinian cause; Palestine, a country they had never set eyes on.

That night I decided to write my will—but as a Sunni Muslim I could not. Our laws were clear: in case of death any possess-ions I might have would be divided between my daughters, my father and my three brothers. I called my stepmother in Switzerland and told her to tell my brothers I relied on their sense of honour to pass anything I owned to my daughters, little though it was. My father came to the phone and reassured me that everything was all right in Lebanon. I was about to give him the harrowing details, but then thought, what's the use? I painted the situation in such glowing colours I nearly convinced him we were on the road to Tel Aviv and he would soon be harvesting his own watermelons! My father, who was no fool, could still sleep a little better that night.

There was another ceasefire. Beirut sighed with relief at the absence of noise. This appeared to be more serious. It had been announced by the Israelis, although they insisted it was an Israeli-Syrian ceasefire, making no mention of the PLO, whose existence they preferred to ignore. (The truce was also accepted by the PLO forces.) We were told this was a prelude to diplomatic negotiations; there was talk of a cabinet of national unity being formed; of an international force that would limit the Syrian and Palestinian presence in Lebanon. What about the Israeli occupation? Later, later, said Washington. The airport was in shambles and two Middle East Airlines (MEA—the Lebanese national carrier) planes had been hit. And Port Stanley was about to fall into the hands of the British. . .

An empty apartment in the children's building had been taken over by twenty-two refugees. 'My God,' I thought, 'That's awful. Armed elements where the children live is not exactly a godsend.' I rushed over there and knocked on the door, to find myself faced by wounded children and distressed women; there was not a man in sight.

'Can I do anything for you?' I found myself saying.

'No thank you,' the accent was definitely Palestinian and the tone not exactly welcoming.

'Don't be scared. I'm with you not against you.' I was still left standing at the doorstep. A little two-year-old girl had her arm swathed in bandages; she looked at me with interest.

'What happened to her?'

'It's a burn, and we can't find a hospital to change her bandage. They are too busy with more seriously wounded people.'

'I can do it,' I said, 'I did volunteer work a long time ago in a hospital where there were many patients suffering from napalm burns.'

She looked at me in disbelief. She was right: it took me two full hours to change the bandage. I was helped by Leyla, who had a bag filled with medicines she'd spent all day preparing in case of an emergency; she'd even painted a red cross on it. There wasn't much conversation between the little girl's mother and myself, although I tried hard to bring her out of her shell.

King Khaled of Saudi Arabia died of a heart attack and a new reign began with a new monarch. I wondered whether this would make any difference to Lebanon and its crisis. Only time would tell.

CHAPTER 6

On Sunday June 13th we finally received news from our friends and family in Doha. Several houses in that residential area had been hit and the inhabitants could only come out of their houses if they carried a white flag, and then only to go to the supermarket. Former Lebanese Prime Minister Salim al-Hoss, who lived in Doha, was interrogated at length. Every house had been searched for weapons and fedayeen.

In desperation, some of the fighters had hidden in the houses, shooting at any moving target. 'Please, please get out,' said one of the inhabitants. 'No, we have to fight to the death,' they replied. 'We don't want to die, for God's sake. Throw your clothes away and your weapons, take what trousers and shirts you need and get out of here.' Seven of them still lay there in the rubble of one of the villas. Two Israeli tanks stood guard over what used to be one of Lebanon's most peaceful and beautiful areas.

My former husband Nabil was white with anger at the news; he was an architect and he had designed one of the loveliest villas in Doha. He let me know his feelings in no uncertain terms when I went to visit the children.

'It's the Palestinians' fault,' he raged, 'They've ruined the country.'

'Will you stop it! I can't stand this any more,' I said, 'Wherever I go I hear nothing but insults. Can't you be reasonable and look at the history to see whose fault it really is, why and how the Palestinians landed in this country?'

He couldn't, and I could understand why not. Lebanon was in a shambles and all he could see before his eyes was an immense fire. He didn't want to listen and I'd had enough insults. Anyway, Leyla was eavesdropping and she looked distraught. Everybody's nerves were cracking, mine included.

I decided to take Leyla and Rasha for a drive through Beirut, or what was left of it, to show them the damage and try to explain why our activities were so restricted this summer. We drove by the seaside, where not one street was without a mountain of sand; you no longer drove down the streets, you executed slaloms.

'Look at the sea, isn't it beautiful?' said Rasha. 'I wish we could swim.' So did I, but all I saw were Israeli battleships on the horizon.

'Let's go and visit your grandmother,' and off we went to see their father's mother. We found their paternal uncle and his family there, who had come from the suburbs of Beirut seeking refuge. I was given a partly friendly, partly hostile welcome. I had no idea how they'd got out alive and didn't dare ask: anything that was even a hundredth part Palestinian wasn't too welcome at this point. I tried to reason with them but in vain; their nerves were shattered.

Those days I tried to put a brave face on things for the children but my mind was in a muddle; I went from tears to laughter with great suddenness; and almost every day I rang people I knew abroad to say farewell. I spoke to my cousin Nadia (who sounded very sad), my cousin Ghada (who laughed at my 'dramatics'), my Aunt Hayat, and my brother Feysal (the one married to an English girl), who sounded serious but quiet. Feysal had just had a novel published in which he announced to all and sundry that he'd always hated my guts. I was hurt but not too concerned; I had other matters to think of at this point. The title of his book was *Castles in Palestine;* I suggested the title of his next should be *Ruins in Lebanon.*

The air raids were becoming heavier and every home in Beirut shook under the impact of the bombardment. Meanwhile, Israeli Chief of Staff Rafael Eitan went to visit his troops at Baabda, seat of the presidential palace. He had a nerve going so close to Lebanon's symbol of legality, however broken the country was. And meanwhile US Secretary of State Alexander Haig put pressure on Israel not to engage in the battle of Beirut unless it was for self-defence! I thought you defended yourself when you were attacked, not when you were the aggressor; Haig should consult a good English dictionary. And meanwhile, the Security Council was called into session again; I didn't think many Lebanese had high hopes of that meeting.

Back in Beirut, the Swiss, the Swedes and the Americans were now advising their citizens to leave (although Haig seemed to think there would be no battle for Beirut). But who could blame the foreigners for leaving when even some West Beirutis had flown the coop.

My little Rasha spent a lot of time listening to adults who didn't notice her presence and was very worried.

'How is Abou Ammar* today?' she asked me. I was taken aback; Rasha didn't know Yasser Arafat and she certainly had never discussed him or any other politician before.

'He's fine, why do you ask?' I queried.

The little nine-year-old explained: 'I heard that every building he goes to is bombed by the Israelis. I also heard that people are scared of that.' I looked at her in surprise; this was news to me, but then out of the mouths of babes. . .

'Do you want him to die?' I asked.

'No!' Rasha replied vehemently.

'Why not?'

'Because.'

'That's not an answer.'

'Because he's Palestinian like you, and I just don't want him to die.' Rasha's political conversation was over; she rushed back to the swings in her grandmother's gardens, and I went back to my daydreaming.

On Monday June 14th, the Spanish joined the Swiss, the Americans, the Germans, the Dutch, the Belgians et al, in the exodus from West Beirut. At any rate the Spanish had more reason to go; after all, the World Cup was waiting. Far away in the Falkland Islands, the Argentines had capitulated and General Galtieri was in a mess.

We hadn't heard much from the Arabs, who didn't seem to give a hoot about the Lebanese and Palestinians, but we did hear from Haig, who said that Beirut would not be occupied, and from Begin, who promised the battles would be over soon. So far 15,000 Lebanese and Palestinian civilians had been killed or wounded. Could it be that Begin found the number insufficient? Was six million his goal? There just weren't that many people in Lebanon.

* PLO chairman Yasser Arafat's *nom de guerre*.

41

'How is Abou Ammar today? ' That was Rasha asking after Arafat again, very much in earnest. I had checked out her story the night before and found it was true. In fact, I'd learned that one day when he was seen entering a building, a whole deputation came and begged him to leave; his answer was a speech on patriotism. I suppose one has to look at history to see that in war only a small part of the population engages in active resistance against the occupier, while the rest are passive resisters or simply resigned to their fate.

That Monday was Leyla and Rasha's first day working as volunteers. They bade me farewell at the door of the Red Cross, and I went off to bid farewell again to all the people I loved and who all seemed to be so far away. My friends made fun of me but they were as white-faced as I was. When I called my father I choked on my tears and had to hand the phone to a friend and tell her to pretend she was me. I was scared, scared for my children, for the Palestinians' future, for Lebanon's fate.

My friend Amal told me to pull myself together. 'I'll get you a cauliflower if you're good,' she said jokingly, knowing I loved fresh cauliflower salad. It was just as well she was joking because there were no more vegetables to be had in our part of the city; there was barely any electricity, very little water, and hardly any diesel, fuel or gas. Supermarket shelves were empty from panic buying, and you had to queue for hours for bread. Some medicines were simply no longer to be found. A woman at the Red Cross had asked me that morning whether I could try to get any anti-gangrene serum from abroad; even cotton and gauze were in very short supply.

Amal had just been listening to the radio and she came rushing in: 'They've formed a Committee of National Salvation!'

'Who have? '

'The Lebanese. It includes Chafic al-Wazzan [the Prime Minister], Bashir Gemayel [the Phalangist leader], Nabih Birri [leader of Amal (the Shia movement)] , as well as Walid Joumblatt, Fuad Boutros [the Foreign Minister] and Nasri Maalouf [the Greek Catholics' representative].'

'What happens to the actual government?' I asked.

'This has nothing to do with that.'

I didn't think this was such a positive development; we had a government, it should deal with the problems. But then no one had asked my opinion. Meanwhile, the Israelis were fighting the Syrians in the Bekaa, in the Chouf and in the Metn; they were fighting the Palestinians, the Lebanese Communists, the Progressives, the Syrians and an assortment of other fighters at Khalde, which was by then known as the Khalde Triangle. The battles were fierce in the Triangle and they'd already lost four tanks. The Israelis back home might not have known it, but their famous Tsahal army seemed to be in a mess. By June 15th (my mother's birthday), the Israeli army had been fighting for twelve days, six more than in the 1967 war. Had Begin, Eitan and Sharon planned on such a long war with the poor, stupid Arabs of Lebanon and Palestine?

Ariel Sharon had 'visited' Baabda that day in full battle-dress and in all his arrogance. I had a message for him. If he had been a good Jew he would have known it because it was from the Bible:

> Ah! you destroyer, yourself undestroyed,
>> betrayer still unbetrayed,
>> when you cease to destroy you will be destroyed,
>> after all your betrayals, you will be betrayed yourself. . .
> Hark, how the valiant cry aloud for help,
>> and those sent to sue for peace weep bitterly!
> The highways are deserted, no travellers tread the roads.
> Covenants are broken, treaties are flouted;
>> man is of no account;
> The land is parched and wilting,
> Lebanon is eaten away and crumbling;
> Sharon has become a desert,
> Bashan and Carmel are stripped bare.
> Now, says the Lord, I will rise up.
> Now I will exalt myself, now lift myself up.
> What you conceive and bring to birth is chaff and stubble;
>> a wind like fire shall devour you.
> Whole nations shall be heaps of white ash,
>> or like thorns cut down and set on fire.
>
> *Isaiah, 33*

I wondered how many Israeli soldiers had died so far and whether this would affect public opinion in Israel in any way; I was counting on it. On another level, I was glad I hadn't held a shekel in my hands, and I hoped I never would. There were now Israeli 'banks on wheels' in the occupied Lebanese territories, complete with telex machines and all.

Rasha had been very right; a former Israeli general, Mattiyahu Peled, said on French television that Begin's intention had been all along to capture Yasser Arafat, take him back to Tel Aviv and try him in public. Another Eichmann—except that Arafat had been a young man in Palestine at the time of Dachau, Auschwitz and Nuremberg.

'How is Abou Ammar?' He was fine, was my answer to her daily question. Leyla had another question for me that day: 'Have we won them yet?' Neither of them wanted to work at the Red Cross any more; they had had enough of counting panadol, valium and aspirin tablets. So I took them to the College Protestant—a French school that had been turned into a headquarters for UNRWA (the UN agency set up to care for the Palestinian refugees in 1949) and the Red Cross.

'They're too young to help here,' the person in charge said.

'Well, they're not too young to die, so they can't be too young to work,' I answered cynically. They took them, and the children loved it: they made cardboard boxes, filled sacks of flour, sugar and powdered milk, shooed away the flies, and waited for me laughing every day at one o'clock.

Begin had gone to Washington to meet Haig and Reagan. Lebanon's President Sarkis could have done the same, but he seemed to be suffering from depression; or was he so protected in his ivory tower that he didn't realise what was happening? Did he know that on the official Radio Lebanon the announcers were not allowed to refer to the Israeli army as 'the enemy' or to the F-15s and F-16s as American-made bombers? Had he any idea what West Beirut looked like since he left his rooms at the Carlton Hotel here in 1976 to assume the presidency? As far as I could remember he had only left his ivory tower twice since the beginning of the invasion, once to visit his home village and once to attend a funeral. Did he realise that one of my children thought Hafez al-Assad was President of Lebanon? Did he know what it felt like to be raided from the air, to be shelled from land and sea, and that car bombs still exploded everywhere as though we hadn't enough problems. 'Come down and see for yourself,' I cried, but I knew he never would.

Meanwhile, the Chileans had joined the Swedes, the Swiss, the Spaniards, the Americans, the Dutch, the Germans and the Italians in the flight from West Beirut. The National Salvation Committee was about to start work: Marwan, who apart from being Minister of Tourism was the National Movement's representative in the cabinet, had gone up to Mukhtara in the American Ambassador's car to bring Walid Joumblatt down to Beirut. Joumblatt was sceptical about the size of the committee and wanted it to include other members like Raymond Eddé (living in exile in Paris), but Marwan persuaded him to give it a try. On their way down from the Chouf, they saw the southern suburbs of Beirut being bombed, as well as the airport and the villages on the road from the mountains. I couldn't help comparing the National Salvation Committee to the Salvation Army I used to see on the streets of New York. All I remembered about the Salvation Army was that it collected old clothes to give to the poor, and its members wore black and prayed a great deal. I hoped our Committee would do a little more for this country.

While Leyla and Rasha filled sacks of flour, I scoured the city for vegetables, fuel and gas, and listened to the radio. I heard that the UN had decided to renew the mandate of UNIFIL (the UN Interim Force in Lebanon), which I thought was very, very funny, since UNIFIL had been stationed as a buffer force on the Lebanese border to keep the Israelis on one side and the Lebanese and Palestinians on the other.

Hebrew signs were everywhere in Lebanon except in the Bekaa, in the North and in West Beirut. Sharon announced that Damascus was within range of his guns and warned the 'terrorists' to throw down their arms. People were being arrested by the thousands in the South and prison camps had been hurriedly erected by the Israeli occupiers, who seemed to have been excellent students of Hitler and all the other murderers in the world. A Canadian doctor and two Norwegian doctors were also arrested on June 13th while working at a Palestinian hospital in Tyre, and their eyewitness account of treatment in the prison camps was horrifying.

'Shalom!' said a man walking past my car.

'Are you talking to me?' I asked in surprise.

'Yes, I said shalom.' He was serious!

'Shut up!' I responded, and my car leaped forward almost of

45

its own accord to show its displeasure. My car had recently been christened by Leyla and Rasha, who had decided to call it 'Aziza' (the beloved); its horn had a name too, 'Sami'. Sami was an eccentric and worked only when he wasn't needed. I was an eccentric too and today I decided not to call anybody up to say goodbye. I was angry: too many people had left West Beirut after the American Embassy's call to its civilians. Many of the Southerners had gone back, no doubt thinking it was safer to be where lightning had already struck; some of those living in badly hit areas of West Beirut had gone to the East, those who could afford it.

While people hunted through West Beirut in search of food for their children, we heard some very interesting conversations on the short-wave radio. A Mrs Halabi, who had clearly recently taken refuge in the East, was busy cooking lobster, shrimp and roast; she had a big dinner party on that night. She couldn't have known what was happening in the place she'd lived in for the last thirty or forty years.

Some had suddenly shown their true colours in the face of the Israeli occupation. One was former Lebanese President Camille Chamoun, who was interviewed by Israeli television at his home in Ashrafiye. What he said went like this: I am afraid the Palestinian forces will not stop fighting; the formation of a strong central government of Christians and Muslims is absolutely necessary; I hope the negotiations will be able to convince the Palestinians to put down their arms; in 1976 when we looked for outside help nobody came; only the Israeli government answered our call.

Chamoun seemed to have forgotten that the Syrians had helped him out when his militia was attacking the Palestinian refugee camp at Tal al-Zaatar; his son Dany who commanded the militia could have reminded him. But then Chamoun had always needed someone's help to reach his goals—the French, the Syrians, the Israelis, the British, to say nothing of the Americans when he was President in 1958 and civil war broke out between the Lebanese. He never turned to the Lebanese for unity, but always to people from other lands. But I no longer held it against him; after all, he had turned eighty-two in April.

It looked like the beginning of a real siege of Beirut. A Red Cross cargo ship, the Anton, carrying medicine for the wounded, was turned back by the Israelis. It was no longer an easy matter to flee to the East—or should I call it the 'liberated area' of Lebanon? This area covered the two thousand square kilometres under the control of Bashir Gemayel's so-called Lebanese Forces, which grouped the Phalangists and other right-wing Christian militias. But who was Gemayel kidding? His forces had long since crushed Chamoun's militia and forced its leader Dany Chamoun to flee with his family for safety—first to Palestinian-controlled areas and then on to Europe. The Lebanese Forces were the Phalangists, pure and simple.

All Lebanese or non-Lebanese who left West Beirut were now stopped at Phalangist barricades. They were thoroughly searched and interrogated, and then either sent back or allowed into the East. Embassies complained to the Lebanese Foreign Ministry about the treatment of their diplomats. But the Lebanese Forces' own 'foreign ministry' issued a statement of explanation: 'The High Command of the Lebanese Forces took a series of measures a few days ago to reinforce security in the liberated areas and to stop the infiltration of all subversive elements. One measure consists of searching all cars at checkpoints, including official and diplomatic cars. Despite the explanations given directly to many of the diplomats, some isolated and regrettable incidents seem to have taken place. . . The Lebanese Forces ask for the understanding and co-operation of all people concerned.' The Lebanese Forces were clearly unaware of diplomatic immunity, as French Ambassador Paul-Marc Henry found when he was searched on his way to the presidential palace at Baabda.

Rasha was unconcerned about the Lebanese Forces, the Communists or any of the others. All she wanted to know was when school would reopen and 'How is Abou Ammar?' And US Secretary of State Alexander Haig assured us yet again that the Israelis would not enter West Beirut—except in self-defence!

CHAPTER 7

It was Sunday, glorious Sunday—but then every day in West Beirut had become a Sunday, with all the shops closed and people in their homes. We couldn't even get our clothes cleaned at a laundry since there was neither electricity nor water. I wore the same shirts every day, hoping that a bit of cologne would do the trick.

The National Salvation Committee met that day with much fanfare; the Range-Rovers, Mercedes and BMWs rolled up to great publicity. Meanwhile, the Danish Embassy announced that it was transferring its headquarters to the East; every time an embassy moved we pretended it was only temporary. West Beirut was being left to stew in its own juice.

Lebanese leaders from various political parties exchanged accusations. Declared Walid Joumblatt: 'Sarkis and Wazzan have disappointed me. They both seem to want to get rid of the Palestinian presence more than the Israeli occupation.' Said Shaikh Pierre Gemayel, founder of the Phalangists and father of Shaikh Bashir: 'The Arabs must divide the Palestinians in Lebanon among them.' He seemed to think they were sacks of flour you could transport here and there. Raymond Eddé declared from his exile in Paris; 'Israel has committed genocide, and the attitude of the president of the Lebanese republic is one of passivity.'

I lay in bed reflecting on the events of the day: the only good news seemed to be Iraq's official announcement that it was withdrawing its troops from Iran. Would this make any difference to us? I was finding it harder and harder to go to sleep. Suddenly a huge explosion rocked the building; it was 3.30 in the morning. What an aid to sleep!

Early the next day I rushed down to find out what the explosion was. It turned out to be sixty kilograms of TNT placed several blocks away and it had nearly destroyed a building on Hamra Street where Nabil's offices were. I rushed down there to see the damage, and found to my relief that although half the building was in ruins Nabil's offices had not been damaged. If they had been he might have blamed it on me! Everybody's nerves were cracking and I kept trying to tell myself not to pay attention to the insults.

Tuesday June 22nd was the first day of Ramadan, the month of fasting for the Muslims and of sympathy with the poor. 'Why fast this year around?' I told a cousin of the children who was fasting and desperately thirsty, 'There's nothing to be had anyway. This year we're the poor, let someone else do the fasting.'

On Wednesday June 23rd Philip Habib seemed to be worried that the truce was breaking down. What truce? I had never heard of a truce that applied to only part of a country; that day it was our turn for a ceasefire, but not the rest. Bhamdoun, a lovely summer resort, had fallen into the hands of the Israelis. Many people had fled the bombing of Beirut to shelter in Bhamdoun, only to be killed or wounded there. Two little boys who used to play with my children at the Golf Club lay wounded by a cluster bomb in Bhamdoun. Sana Najjar had graduated only last year and her graduation had been a double celebration with her wedding. She now lay dead and buried in the ruins of her home. Sana was neither a fighter nor a 'terrorist'; she was Lebanese and a landscape architect.

The French announced their departure that Tuesday, an indication that things were really serious. On the practical side of life, we were allowed four hours of electricity a day and four hours of water after international pressure on the Israelis— but the electricity and water never came on at the same time so it was impossible to run the motors to fill the water tanks on the roofs of West Beirut. Phone lines between East and West were cut.

I took the children to their grandmother's, where there was a generator and where they could have a proper bath and sit in lit rooms. At 5.45 that afternoon the house was suddenly rocked to its foundations by an explosion; we literally saw the walls sway before our eyes. Leyla put her hands to her eyes and screamed in pain; I rushed to her in panic. 'It's an explosion,' one of the bodyguards at the house announced somewhat unnecessarily. Leyla was not hurt, but I was still upset. None of our friends had called to find out if we were all right. I found out later that my friends were upset with me for the same reason. Every person living in West Beirut had had the impression that the explosion was on their doorstep. It turned out to have been nowhere near any of us: 425 kilograms of TNT had been placed in a truck near the Phoenicia Hotel on the seafront. Two buildings were completely flattened, and 145 refugees from the South who had taken shelter there were killed or wounded; the cries of those buried alive continued through the night; some of the bodies had been hurled into the sea by the force of the blast; every window within one kilometre had been shattered. It had been such a quiet, peaceful day that

Tuesday: the residential areas had just been bombarded a few times, and only 25 people had been killed and 75 wounded. That was our truce.

Menahem Begin was back from Washington and had called for a cabinet meeting. Had Washington given them a green light? Was the battle of Beirut about to begin? Philip Habib waited impatiently for the answers, but the Israelis continued to insist that the Palestinians should lay down their arms, and the Palestinians continued to insist on an Israeli pullback before they did so. As the days went by, we were bombed from all fronts and the sky; nothing was spared in our baptism of fire and blood.

Israeli bombers dropped leaflets on us one day, intended not for the Lebanese but for the Syrian soldiers and addressed to their commander Brigadier Muhammad Hallal. The leaflets invited him and his remaining forces to leave Beirut and provided a map showing the way out; a pass was attached to give them safe exit. I ignored the leaflets but that afternoon I noticed that many of the Syrian barricades we had got so used to over the last six years had gone. I kind of missed them!

Later I gave way to my feelings of panic and went to the children's house shaking and scared, no longer knowing what to do or what to think. There was no water again, no electricity, no vegetables, meat, bread or yoghurt. French Foreign Minister Claude Cheysson weighed in on our side and accused Reagan of being totally in the hands of the Israelis. Tel Aviv 'disqualified' France from playing a role in the conflict: but this wasn't a football game, though maybe the Israelis thought it was.

Everybody's nerves were on edge—hence a huge fight with Nabil; he wanted me to take the children and leave. I didn't want to run away, and insisted he take them out. Finally we decided to arrange for their departure to Doha as a first step, then to my brother Feysal's in England. I called him up to ask him to take care of them, but could hardly speak for sobbing. I tried to pull myself together: what had happened to the courageous woman I had been, who lived through the civil war of 1975-76 with nerves of steel? Except that this was different, this was a regular army which hit from afar and never saw its victims, not the small militias of the civil war; and this was an army that did not give a damn. I froze every time the fighter bombers flew over us; Leyla and Rasha thought the look on my face was very funny.

'Are you scared?' they asked.

'No!'

'Then let's play monopoly.'

Later that evening Walid Joumblatt declared that the PLO 'should capitulate and the Palestinians must leave Beirut'. We froze to hear this from the leader of the National Movement which was fighting alongside the PLO. He went on to explain that 'Arafat is trying to gain time, hoping for a miracle in the Arab world, but I don't believe it will happen. The PLO needs a new command.' Was that declaration really necessary, I wondered, or was it said in frustration or anger? Didn't we have enough problems?

Somebody decided to introduce a new element into the war: an ambulance was given as a present to the people of Amal (the Shia militia) in the Beirut suburb of Chiyah. As one of the officials opened it, the white ambulance blew sky-high; two dead, 12 wounded.

On Friday June 25th, I dropped the children off at the College Protestant where they still went to give a hand. When I picked them up at lunch-time every day, they smelt of milk and flour and had dirty faces and hands, but they were happy with their achievements. I thanked God for the sweetness of their nature, for their courage and perseverance. I left them there and went hunting for vegetables and fuel. It was funny, but one could still find vegetables if one looked hard enough.

'Where do you get them from?' I asked the Kurd at his stall.

'From the East.'

'But the Israelis are blocking all the entrances from the East,' I said.

'I know, but we pay them a little something and they let us pass.' That was good to know—the Israelis were just as corruptible as we were. I paid for the vegetables and went off in search of fuel. I was told there was a station near the Phoenicia Hotel that had some and nobody dared go because of the explosion; I was told to carry a gallon container because they didn't allow cars near the place for fear of car bombs.

I went on foot and queued; there were some forty people ahead of me. After an hour in the heat I was dripping but happy; it was my turn at last.

'No more today, come back tomorrow,' said the attendant;

51

there was no arguing with him, so I went.

I walked back to my car and went off to the Ministry of Tourism in Sanayeh where Walid Joumblatt was about to give a press conference. The place was packed with foreign correspondents. Joumblatt seemed nervous but firm, pacing up and down the office. When everyone was there, he announced that he had decided to withdraw from the National Salvation Committee: 'The Americans and Israelis want to annihilate the Palestinians. . . We're not given a chance to have a ceasefire for negotiations. The Palestinians are ready to put down their guns, but they want an honourable withdrawal, plus guarantees for their future. . . There have been no guarantees so far from the United States or Israel. . . I refuse to pursue the negotiations under the pressure of the Israeli war machine. . . I intend to stay here in West Beirut.' He also accused Arabs and Westerners alike of being involved in the conspiracy. Joumblatt was wise not to bow to pressure and a true leader in his determination to stay on in West Beirut.

Two Druze ministers left the Lebanese government in the wake of Walid Joumblatt's resignation from the Committee, Khaled Joumblatt and Marwan Hamade. They were counting on the resignation of a couple of others as well, but these had moved bodily to the East side, and no one was sure what they would do. In the meantime, the Prime Minister, Chafic Wazzan, emerged from a meeting with President Sarkis to announce that he was resigning as well: he no longer believed in the Americans' good will or the Israelis' wish for peace. Washington's response? 'No comment'.

We heard that the Arabs were preparing for a summit meeting. I had no faith in that; all I had faith in were those who stayed in West Beirut. Should I have been so angry with those who had left? Voice of Israel Radio had been advising the people of West Beirut to clear out, every hour on the hour. I was reminded of 1948, when the Palestinians were told to leave, that the war would be over soon, that their lands would be freed for them. The West Beirutis who had stayed had no wish to go anywhere; they'd learned from other people's mistakes.

It was the twenty-second day of the war, and the Israelis had begun to worry. Sharon told them daily that they'd won the war, but some answered sceptically: 'A snake that's been

52

hit on the tail is not a dead snake; what about the head?' The official number of Israeli casualties issued by the Ministry of Defence was 209 dead. *Haaretz* announced that 275 Israeli soldiers had died in Lebanon; at the same time, it had placed 425 obituaries in its inside pages as the days went by. That was a huge number for Israel; I wondered if they compared it to our 15,000 dead and wounded.

Resignations come in threes: that Friday we learnt of Alexander Haig's resignation. We heard that he and President Reagan made the announcement together, their faces very pale. Was this good or bad news? At any rate Haig had not exactly been on our side, so I was not sorry to see him go.

There was joy in West Beirut when people heard of Haig's departure—'Haig the Menace' had gone—and hope at the arrival of George Shultz as Secretary of State. There was also joy at the news of the anti-war demonstration in Israel attended by one hundred thousand people.

The days went by, each very much like the one before. We kept being told that Begin's 'patience had its limits' as his army stood at the entrance of West Beirut, and that if negotiations didn't get the PLO out soon. . . The Israelis controlled the Beirut-Damascus highway; the Bekaa was in turmoil; President Mubarak of Egypt advised the PLO not to leave Lebanon; and, still, every time there was a Security Council resolution for an Israeli withdrawal it was vetoed by the Americans for not being 'even-handed'. What was one to think of the Americans? I liked the American people. But what was their administration trying to do to us? To annihilate everybody, using Israel, in order to arrive at a 'just, peaceful and lasting settlement' in the Middle East?

Between Friday and Sunday, 209 people were killed in Beirut and 150 in the mountains; 153 were wounded in Beirut, and 200 in the mountains. A journalist on the French daily *L'Orient-Le Jour* wrote this account of his trip through the mountains:

It is a horrendous tour beginning at the Jamhour barricade which has been turned over by the Syrians to the Lebanese Army. . . A little farther on is the barricade of the Lebanese Forces; alongside are two abandoned Syrian tanks. At the next corner, just before Araya, lies the charred corpse of a

Syrian soldier, beside his smouldering tank. . . Right after Araya, you go through another barricade and pass a church where the funeral of an air raid victim is taking place. . . All the buildings along the road have been destroyed by Israeli raids. . .

In Aley, Israeli tanks are parked on both sides of the road. A little further up is an Israeli barricade where your identity card is checked in total silence. . . We see the slow advance of 40 Israeli tanks on their way to clean up the area. In Bhamdoun there is nothing but burned vehicles and tanks. Israeli soldiers are everywhere, preventing journalists from taking pictures, especially of those prisoners being taken away with their eyes blindfolded. Corpses lie everywhere, burned by phosphorous bombs; some of them are nonchalantly picked up and deposited on trucks for eventual burial in a common grave.

The road to Sofar is closed. An Israeli soldier who refuses to divulge his name explains: the road is closed because tanks are arriving from Sidon on their way to Beirut to participate in the battle for the capital in case we decide to go ahead with it.

L'Orient-Le Jour, Sunday July 27th.

It was absolutely reassuring to read all that in the morning paper. I picked Leyla and Rasha up at one and took them for lunch at the Myrtom House, an Austrian restaurant which was still functioning and where they could have cold apple juice. There were a few journalists here and there, and then Walid Joumblatt walked in. Rasha got very excited, claiming she'd seen that gentleman before. I whispered his name in her ear, and her eyes popped out of her head; she'd never seen a real, live personality before, she whispered back.

We played a general knowledge contest, with Leyla quickly losing interest because Rasha kept giggling; my daughters both knew the name of the Saudi King and not of the President of Lebanon. Rasha started pelting me with questions in exchange:

'Who invented the word for table?'

'I don't know.'

'Who found names for people?'

'I have no idea.'

'Why is the world round?'

'Hmm, now let me see. . .'

'I bet you don't know. Here, shall I read you your horoscope?' She and I were both Aquarians.

'A great day for leisure time,' Rasha read, 'for sports, exercise and success in business. You are about to receive good news from abroad.'

'Sure, an Israeli bash on the head all the way from Tel Aviv.' Rasha found that very funny. Our conversation turned serious. I told her that twenty thousand people had demonstrated in our support in Nicaragua.

'Well, that's nice of Nicaragua,' she said, 'I'll help them when I grow up.' I told her about Haig and Shultz; did that mean they could go to Camp Kiniya this summer after all? I changed the subject. Yesterday was 'Shabat Shalom' in Israel, but we had had no peace here.

Ismat, my friend and lunch companion of the past couple of years, no longer knew what to do with herself. Should she leave? Should she stay on principle? She and her family had already moved out of their home to a safer area; she worked for the Economic Commission for Western Asia, and could easily be transferred to Baghdad if she chose.

'Should I stay or leave?' she asked.

'Leave.'

'I don't want to leave.'

'Well, then, stay.'

'I'm scared.'

'Then leave.'

'I don't want to leave. My parents, my friends. . . I just don't want to leave. . .'

That conversation went on until I lost patience and offered to take her to lunch at the Myrtom House (again) with Irene. I took the children to their grandmother's and off we went. They had cabbage salad at the Myrtom House, which was quite an achievement. Each table had a radio on it. You could tune in to the official Radio Lebanon—and the other Lebanese factions' radios that had gone on the air during the civil war: Radio Free Lebanon, Radio Voice of Lebanon, Radio Voice of Arab Lebanon—as well as Radio Monte Carlo, the Voice of Israel, the BBC, the Voice of America. We listened to everybody to find out where we stood. Briefly, Tel Aviv wanted the resistance transformed into a political movement; the Palestinians hinted they had agreed to depart in principle, but wanted a multinational force to stand between them and the Israelis as they left; the Israelis refused; the White House admitted to a link between Haig's departure and the 'Lebanese crisis'. President Sarkis opened his mouth at last and told us Lebanon was going through difficult times; he talked about the history of Lebanon and its tolerance; he even mentioned the Israeli invasion, and pleaded for help from the Arab kings and presidents to save Beirut. Ismat could stay now!

Suddenly a couple of foreign correspondents ran in, all excited and red in the face, brandishing a couple of blue leaflets. 'Does anyone here know Arabic? Does anybody here know Arabic?' It sounded as if they were asking 'Is there a doctor in the house?'

'I do.' They gave me the leaflet and I translated it, pausing from time to time to look at the faces around me that were slowly turning white. The leaflets, dropped from the sky by the Israelis, advised the West Beirutis to leave to ensure their safety and that of their loved ones; they were told to head East or to take the Beirut-Damascus highway. The Israelis were on their way. The leaflet was numbered 26; no doubt the other 25 had been dropped on the heads of those in Tyre, Sidon, Nabatieh, Aley, Bhamdoun, and so on. We left the restaurant and took Ismat back to her car. As she was walking from my car to hers, there was an ear-splitting explosion: two cars blew up and flew sky-high. The air was filled with smoke and glass, with screams and cries for help. I could see Ismat on the street, her hands pressed to her ears. For a second I forgot she was my friend and wanted to drive away, but only for a second. I turned around and drove up to her, opened the door and told her to get in; she was in a state of shock and frozen to the spot, so I had to shout at her.

She got in and we drove away like madwomen. I later discovered that those two cars had belonged to friends of mine. They had just stepped inside the building; two people had been killed and twenty-one wounded.

At the children's grandmother's in Musseitbeh, one could have written a treatise on panic. The leaflets had certainly done their work well. Only Leyla seemed to be amused. She told me a bag had dropped out of the sky and burst open on the ground, and out had spilled thousands and thousands of pieces of paper. She didn't touch them, they could be poisoned, couldn't they? She imitated her aunt who, five minutes later, ran out of the house screaming at everybody, pushed her three small children into a car, and drove South. Thousands of people seemed to be doing the same.

'We're not leaving, are we?' Leyla asked.

'No, we're not,' I answered firmly. This was psychological warfare and I hated it. I wasn't going to be scared into packing up and going.

One of the first to leave was the Prime Minister's right-hand man. He took his beloved spouse to spend the summer of '82 at the smart Printania Hotel in Broummana, up in the mountains. The Prime Minister was furious; a few months earlier he had fought a long battle to have this man appointed. Another of those who went East was a high-ranking official in a Druze commission; it didn't take him long to take his wife and child to the clean, healthy air of the mountains, where he continued to issue orders. Everybody made fun of him. Another was an important member of the Mourabitoun (the Lebanese Nasserite movement), who insisted he'd been sent on official business to Tripoli via Damascus. He'd liked it here when the going was good, when there was dancing, laughing and dinners.

A former member of the Mourabitoun had tried to send his wife and children off to France, but they were turned back at Ashrafiye. We made fun of him, but he took it very nicely. The big question among the West Beirutis who stayed was:

'Are they leaving or aren't they leaving?'

'Who?'

'The Palestinians, of course.'

'What about the Israelis?'

'Oh, they'll leave eventually.'

Things have really been turned topsy-turvy; the Israelis had invaded and they wanted the Palestinians to leave first. Where was the logic in all of this? Meanwhile, a new joke was making the rounds: 'Abou Ammar is holding an urgent meeting when he hears a lot of shouting outside. "What's happening?" he asks. "We don't know", comes the answer. "Go and check." One of his bodyguards comes rushing back in excitement: "Abou Ammar, Abou Ammar, there are 450,000 West Beirutis who have come here to bid you and the PLO farewell". "Why?"

asks Abou Ammar, "Where are they going?" ' We told this story a thousand times over and shouted with laughter each time.

We forgot about the leaflets and played hide and seek. That evening I had another big argument with Nabil; I didn't want Leyla and Rasha to leave. I delighted in their company, and they gave me courage and fortitude. Leyla heard the whole discussion from her corner. She took me into her room and cried softly: 'I don't want to leave, I'm happy here.' 'Don't worry,' I said, 'You're not going anywhere. Don't worry.'

CHAPTER 8

'Have we won them yet, Mummy?' Leyla asked excitedly on Monday June 28th. I wished we all had her optimism. The descriptions of the scene at the home for the aged and mentally handicapped, badly shelled by the Israelis the previous Friday, were horrifying. Lebanese of all ages and religions lay stunned in the shambles of that institution that had housed twelve hundred already helpless people. 'During World War II people were not so crazy,' said an old man of seventy-five from the bed he'd stayed in during the shelling.

That Monday afternoon the Israeli jets roared overhead and released thousands of white leaflets. Leaflet number 27 had no effect on me; I expected that the next day would bring yellow leaflets so we could cut Stars of David out of them and pin them on our T-shirts. We had become blasé about the leaflets very quickly; in Lebanon it didn't take long to get used to this kind of novelty. Much of the panic had subsided since yesterday, but not Ismat's; she left that morning. And a few other people left West Beirut, too, although Shimon Peres, the Israeli Labour Party leader, said that 'entering West Beirut would be a historical error'. The Likud Government claimed the Palestinians were soon to leave by sea. 'How,' asked Arafat, 'on the "Loveboat"?' I remembered how fifteen years ago the Israelis used to scream that the Arabs were throwing them into the sea; now it seemed that fate awaited the Palestinians.

The bombardment continued, and all the buildings Arafat visited received a special gift from the Israeli messengers of peace. We were told this again at the children's grandmother's, who lived in the same building as her brother, former Lebanese Prime Minister Saeb Salam. Amid the constant hustle and bustle, there was a sudden screech of brakes outside, car doors banged and armed men were everywhere. 'It's Abou Ammar,' Rasha said excitedly. He had come to discuss the situation with Saeb Salam. 'Then let's get out of here,' I said jokingly, 'before we get it on the head.' In fact, I had another vodka-orange to drink his health from where I sat; no Israeli was going to scare me out of my wits! When Yasser Arafat left Saeb Salam's Musseitbeh residence, he declared Israel had not yet ended its invasion. In fact, that day Sharon made us a solemn promise: he would annihilate the PLO unless it left the country, but they could take their individual firearms with them.

There was still no electricity or water, and we were drowning in refuse; but on Wednesday June 30th we were suddenly flooded with vegetables. There was nowhere for the rubbish to go so it had to stay—but where were the vegetables coming from? Everything from cabbage, cauliflower, squash, tomatoes, parsley, oranges—to watermelon!

We were blockaded from all sides; nothing could be coming from the East so it must logically be coming from the South. And it was—65,000 dollars worth of Israeli produce a day. The Khalde Triangle had fallen, after fierce resistance that filled the air with the smell of victory despite the smoke of defeat: a regular army had marched up and been held off for days by the Syrians, the Palestinians and most of all the Lebanese (the Progressives, the Communists, the Amal Shia movement). It was only after the Israelis had advanced beyond this point that they were able to 'export' their vegetables to us. I had finally found my watermelon again, but I was not about to buy any, if only to honour those who had fallen at Khalde.

While some of us fought for our honour and dignity, others held a grand meeting in the occupied mountain town of Aley. Some Druze in the mountains who called themselves Lebanese leaders opened their arms to their Druze 'brothers' in Israel, namely a member of the Knesset and a representative of the Druze Shaikh Akl (the name given to their religious leaders) of Israel. Half the Druze religious headquarters in West Beirut was blown into thin air in response.

After the leaflets, we were treated to simulated air raids.

Fortunately they didn't wake up Leyla and Rasha—I personally was terrified. And from our friendly neighbour Israel we received another message: they wanted the total disarmament of Beirut and they were backed by Washington. It was 'no' to a symbolic PLO presence in Beirut, but Philip Habib could have a few more days to negotiate. Thank you, Israel, and thank you President Reagan for not giving the green light for an invasion of West Beirut. Seeing what it was like now, I wondered what it would have been like if you had.

Walid Joumblatt said 'no' to a unilateral disarmament (how right he was); Saeb Salam said 'no' to the removal of the Palestinians; Riyadh said 'no', it had not proposed an evacuation of the fedayeen; Camille Chamoun said 'no', the Palestinians couldn't go to the Bekaa; Israel said 'no', there hadn't been that many civilian victims, just a couple of hundred; Nahib Berri said 'no' to the disarmament of the Muslim Progressives; former premier Yitzhak Rabin said 'no' to a unilateral Israeli withdrawal; and Libya's President Qaddafi urged us to offer our blood as the fuel for resistance—would he like to join us with his?

'Have we won them yet, Mummy?'

'How is Abou Ammar?' My children were sometimes adorable, if I say so myself. It was 8.30 in the morning and they were already dressed and ready to go. Their school had long since been occupied by the Israelis, who by now had reached the famous 'rubbish dump' that the children had found so funny. Our days had settled into a routine: volunteer work for them in the morning, while I hunted for fuel and food; visits to their grandmother's in the afternoon where our political discussions often turned to raging quarrels. But life was good so long as you had dignity and honour.

On the political level, there was one major event that July 1st: the Saudis sent for Bashir Gemayel. But why were they giving him so much importance? They even sent a private plane to bring him to Taef where a small-scale Arab meeting was in progress. Well, one hoped for the best.

The Israeli occupiers' arrogance surpassed all bounds: they had begun to hold press conferences in Beirut itself. Ariel Sharon paid a visit to the Hotel Alexandre in East Beirut, where he invited the Lebanese to fight the Palestinian presence in Lebanon, promising Israel would not keep one inch of

Lebanese territory. He seemed to have forgotten the corpses of Lebanese and Palestinian civilians he had stepped on to reach that hotel.

The last remaining obstacle in the negotiations seemed to be the symbolic military presence in Beirut the PLO was asking for. Now had I been the PLO I would have refused to leave Beirut at that point. Fedayeen had died by the hundreds trying to enter the occupied territories; should they run away now that their enemy had come in search of them? Where were they to go: Egypt, Syria, Jordan? Back to the zero point of 1948? Why should they believe in guarantees? I understood the West Beirutis' feelings and their frustration and anger at seeing their lovely city destroyed—but hadn't they also seen what Israeli occupation meant whatever the promises?

I heard Jane Fonda had visited Israeli and Lebanese wounded in Tel Aviv: how grand of Ms Fonda. Why didn't she come and see what was happening here? Wouldn't she like to have a look at what cluster bombs did, the effect of phosphorous bombs? Wouldn't she like to pay a visit to the Lebanese refugees in the only public garden of West Beirut, to see their anguish and misery at first hand?

It was Saturday July 3rd, 'Shabat Shalom' again. Some of the journalists in West Beirut were getting ready to leave after writing their stories; colleagues were coming to replace them. Lucky them! But I was not leaving: this was my country and nobody was going to get me out, no matter what the price.

On Sunday July 4th, I remembered last year when Leyla and Rasha were at Camp Kiniya in Vermont. That very day they had witnessed the celebrations of America's independence and were happy, so very happy. I wished to God it was last year, for my children's sake, for all the children's sake. I wished we could celebrate our own independence.

'Mummy, are we going to go to Camp Kiniya?'

'I don't know, darling.'

'I wish we could go today.' So did I.

What was Lebanon's Fourth of July like? Let an American citizen in Beirut describe it, Dr Amal Shamma, the slim dark-haired woman who continued to try and run the Barbir Hospital against all odds, to provide some basic treatment for the wounded. Her courage and perseverance became a byword in

West Beirut. She addressed this letter to her President:

Mr Ronald Reagan,
President of the United States of America,
The White House,
1600 Pennsylvania Avenue,
Washington D.C., U.S.A.

Dear Mr Reagan,

This is just a personal letter to hope you had a happy Fourth of July. Let me tell you about mine. I spent my day working with men and women and children who were injured or maimed by bombs made by us back home. It was hectic as usual, especially since I'm not quite sure how to deal with the personal tragedies of others.

The evening was very stimulating. Our water and electricity have been cut off, all the better to see the real live fireworks in the sky. You should have been here to watch them. I'm sure you've never seen anything like it in your life—certainly not back home. There were flare bombs to light up the sky, great explosions all over the horizon, red rockets that blazed across the sky in such wonderful formations and made such great noise. It was a great show and we are promised more to come.

I wanted some of my patients to watch the fireworks with me but they couldn't. Salwa Ikbani is only 14 years old and she has lost seven brothers and sisters, her aunt, cousins, both eyes, and has been in coma for the past 12 days. I doubt she knows what's going on. Inas Shaaban was 1½ years. She would have enjoyed the show but she was burned severely and died last night. Anna Kassir would have enjoyed it, but I couldn't get her out of bed. She's lost both her legs and her daughter and her mother, her sister, and her nieces. She wasn't in the mood for fun. Hassan Hodrog wanted so much to see the fireworks, but he was burned by napalm and didn't make it. Yousef Sayed had just lost his wife and nine children and felt that out of respect, he shouldn't join in the fun just yet.

Some of my patients asked me why we were being honoured by all the special festivities. Somebody mentioned that some of these fireworks were banned not only by

American law, but by international law also. Someone even remembered that America used to claim that it opposes the use of such forceful displays by anybody, friend or foe, to achieve political gains. Argentina was punished for invading the Falklands, Poland for enforcing martial law, Russia for invading Afghanistan, and so on and so forth. It seemed strange to him that when the use of force was so much more violent as it has been in this country, that America would not stand by its convictions. I told him that we were in no position to judge: that only politicians know right from wrong.

Another person asked me about American arithmetic. He couldn't understand how come safe borders for one country were equivalent to the occupation of half of another, the killing of over 14,000, the maiming of tens of thousands, the displacing of hundreds of thousands, the destruction of historic towns and cities, the placing of half a city of two million under siege. I told him that only American policy-makers understand modern math.

Anyway, it has been a most stimulating Fourth of July, especially when I try to explain to people around me why we celebrate the independence of a nation that preaches peace, freedom, justice, and equal rights for all peoples on the face of this earth.

All of us here send you our best and wish you were with us.

> Sincerely yours,
> Amal Shamma, M.D.,
> (a very proud American)

Prime Minister Chafic Wazzan was as obstinate as the West Beirutis: he refused to go and meet Lebanon's President unless the Israelis withdrew from the main road that led to Baabda.

Someone told us a story that morning about Ariel Sharon's arrival at Baabda to visit his troops. Sharon was said to have asked for a glass of water and exclaimed: 'This water is good, where's it from?'

'From the Ain Baabda Spring,' he was told.

'My God, why did you tell him about Baabda's water,' one Lebanese whispered to the other, 'he already knows about the Litani River and look what he did to that!'

In West Beirut we still had no water, Baabda, Litani or otherwise. We still had a bit of bombing (skirmishes they called them), and a lot of refuse. We were beginning to feel the weight of the siege. People barely talked to one another. Leyla and Rasha quarrelled constantly, although they had it so much easier than others. Nabil had installed a generator that had really changed their lives; now they could watch television in the evenings. Little Leyla was put in charge of the generator; she turned it on and off and took care of the fuel I provided.

On the political level, things seemed to have reached stalemate again, and Israel had given Philip Habib until Friday to solve the Palestinian problem. Generous Israel! I supposed we would have another round on that famous day.

Although Philip Habib often met Israeli officers on Lebanese soil, he had never done so at the American Embassy, despite what the press said, or at the Ambassador's residence. Ambassador Dillon was a diplomat and a gentleman and no Israeli had, to my knowledge, entered the Embassy's gates. Thank God for that bit of decency.

If the 5th was Monday, Tuesday must be July 6th—unless the Israelis had decided to stop time as well. The 32nd day of the war and the Israeli people couldn't believe their eyes: Israel's military supremacy had never allowed anyone to fight them for such a long time. The Israelis decided to speed things up a little: a deluge of fire showered down on West Beirut and its southern suburbs. In the meantime they lost men on the battlefield and behind their lines. We didn't have to worry about accounting for our dead, but they did; could they stand the loss much longer?

Early that day I found a baby on the children's doorstep, a lovely baby girl, barely a few hours old. The children were very excited.

'Are you going to keep her, Mummy?'

'Sure, for the time being anyway. She's lovely. Doesn't she look a bit like Rasha?'

'I don't know, but she's cute,' Leyla said tenderly. 'Can I hold her?' What was I going to do with a baby at this point? Who were her parents? Where were they?

'She's so quiet. Is she breathing?' asked Rasha, who had seen nothing but death around her for the past seven years.

'She's sleeping. Don't worry, she's fine.' What was I going

to do with a baby, dear God? First, get her a few things. What did a baby need? Shampoo, nappies, milk, bottles. . . No baby had ever been taken for walks at such a young age, but this one went willingly. Leyla and Rasha took it in turns to hold her. The West Beirutis teased us.

'I didn't know you were pregnant,' they joked.

'I wasn't!'

'Didn't know you had remarried.'

'I haven't.'

'Who is she?'

'I don't know, but I'm beginning to like her.' Who said one could only love one's own baby? Adoption is not such a bad idea, a ready-made baby. But where was her mother? Why didn't she want her?

We discovered her grandparents that evening: the building's doorman and his wife. The baby's father had repudiated her mother, and the grandparents didn't want the child since they planned to remarry their daughter, who had been told the baby was born dead. Her former husband had already remarried and gone South. We struck a bargain. We would look after her during the day and they would have her at night.

'What are you going to call her?' I asked.

'Mouna,' said the grandmother.

'Mouna, my eye! Mouna means heart's desire and nobody wants her. What do you want to call her Mouna for?'

'What do you think we should call her?'

'Saria.'

'What does that mean?'

'Saria, a woman who follows the stars all alone in the desert.' Saria it was; I hoped she would be happy when she grew up, if she did grow up.

Wednesday saw a great wave of optimism; negotiations had reached a final stage in Beirut, Riyadh, Paris and Cairo; an American plan had been approved. I didn't know if the PLO approved it, but the Israelis certainly gave it a great deal of importance by repeating it on the radio every hour on the hour. It was a nine-point plan that provided for Israeli withdrawal by a few kilometres from around Beirut; evacuation of Palestinian forces, who could take their individual weapons; American naval units would safeguard the evacuation by sea; the Palestinian forces would go first to the Syrian port of Latakia then on to other countries; a Franco-American force would take up positions in Beirut; the Lebanese army would enter the Western part of the capital; a stable and sovereign Lebanese government would result; the PLO would maintain political representation in Lebanon; two small units of the Palestine Liberation army would be integrated into the Lebanese army until all foreign forces were evacuated.

It sounded great, but I would believe it when I saw it. Meanwhile, there was a spate of kidnapping: a bishop and ten others were kidnapped in Baalbak; six members of the Lebanese Red Cross were abducted in the mountains and released a few hours later; the First Counsellor at the Iranian Embassy disappeared; and a few others were kidnapped and reappeared as corpses.

In the South, the Israelis continued to erect camps for the prisoners. From Bonn, survivors of Nazi concentration camps sent a letter to the Knesset to protest against Begin's war in Lebanon: 'Stop the bloodshed and withdraw behind the frontiers of the State of Israel. . . stop the carnage.' It was signed by many people, including Bernt Engelmann, president of the Federation of German writers, and Max Oppenheimer, president of the Federation of Anti-Fascists, both survivors of Dachau.

Soviet leader Leonid Brezhnev suddenly got worked up—we hadn't heard his voice before. He warned Reagan mildly against sending an American contingent to Lebanon. Begin told Philip Habib there was no time limit to his mission, but France feared the battle of Beirut was about to begin. The siege went on; some people crossed by foot from West to East, and there was a 'little' shooting in the southern suburbs. Who were we to believe? What were we to do?

We heard the Palestinians were no longer going to leave by sea, but by land through the Bekaa. What did the world think the Palestinians were: sacks of flour or potatoes to be put into trucks and sent on their way? Baby Saria was doing fine: she slept most of the day and kept everybody awake at night. Was she an angel by day and a devil by night? No, she was simply Saria, following her star by night. Her grandparents wanted to change her name to something else so that maybe she would sleep! Leyla, Rasha, Saria and I always went out together; we told each other stories and never discussed politics. In the rest of Lebanon everybody of consequence delivered insults to

66

everybody else of consequence: that was very reassuring for the future unity of Lebanon.

On Friday we heard Damascus didn't want to receive the fedayeen. That was strange—I thought they adored them! The only other thing I remember about that Friday was that night became day. Israel seemed to have its own red phone to God. There were flares everywhere, phosphorous bombs, cluster bombs and all the rest to provide Beirut with its own special daylight.

We heard that the Israelis had taken over the Lebanese army barracks in Beiteddine in the Chouf and handed it over to the Lebanese Forces (ie the Phalangists). Israel had always called for a strong Lebanese army and central government, so why had they kicked it out of its barracks? Somebody else would have to provide the answer: I'd become confused since night turned to day.

CHAPTER 9

Today is July 11th, 1982—or it it July 10th? I don't know any more. My mind is not fixed on the past any longer but on the present as I listen to the world outside coming to an end. I lie half-dressed on my bed, willing my feet to move, to take me to the shelter downstairs, to put heavier walls between me and that shattering noise before I become part of an explosion. But my mind has a more urgent task: it is pulling at its roots, pulling away from me to where there's a sky above the one that's raining bombs on us. I search frantically through my bedroom for pen and paper, thinking only if I write these lines, my mind will stay with me. I start writing. . .

The phone rings, unexpected and shrill in all that thundering noise.

'Can I come and watch television at your place tonight?' a friend asks.

'What? In the middle of this catastrophe? What do you want to watch anyway, "Dallas"?' I answer.

'No, no, "Dallas" is over and done with. I want to watch the Mundial,' she says.

'What Mundial?'

'You know, the World Cup, the football game.'

'Oh that!' I exclaim.

'What do you mean, "Oh, that"? Do you know that the Israeli soldiers are going to take shifts in an organised relay at their posts to be able to watch it?'

'Well, that's good to know. Maybe they'll have less time for us,' I answer sarcastically.

'So can I come and watch it at your place?'

'I don't have any electricity.' She hangs up angrily.

The Italians leave Spain with shouts of victory. Back in Beirut we sit at home in a state of total stupor: we can't believe it's quiet again on the Western front. My ears are still ringing from the noise, and I don't think all the valium in the world will be enough to soothe our panic. Leyla and Rasha reassure me the next day: there was 'only a bit of shooting' yesterday, they say laughingly. I had spent all day on the phone on Sunday trying to reach their house to make sure they were all right; some day of rest that was. We decide to visit their grandmother's, where their aunt, all nerves and haggard-looking, barely smiles at them. She wants to know the news.

'All I know is that Reagan didn't like what happened yesterday,' I reassure her. 'Isn't that a good piece of news? He even gave Begin a scolding. Let's watch the news on television since you have electricity.'

We wait quietly to see yesterday's destruction on the screen— but all we get are films of the presidential palace in the East which has been hit by a few shells from the West. What happened to West Beirut? Maybe it wasn't bombarded yesterday; maybe all that was only a dream, a nightmare. Only the symbol of legality has been hit, if we are to believe the television. Camille Chamoun comes out on the doorstep of Baabda, having visited the President, and gives a delicate hint of encouragement to the Israelis to begin the 'battle of Beirut'. I don't understand anything any more: is he with the Lebanese or against them? Or are the inhabitants of West Beirut simply not Lebanese any more?

Another funny story made the rounds in Beirut that day, of a woman called Valentine Nassar, from Tyre. Her son, Ammar, a member of Saiqa (the pro-Syrian Palestinian group), was caught and imprisoned by the Israeli army. Valentine went to Tel Aviv all the way from Tyre, raised hell and got him out. Ammar, born and bred a Shia Muslim, was found to be originally Jewish because his mother Valentine was Jewish. Not only was Ammar released from jail, but he was now fighting with the Israeli army!

Monday July 12th is a fresh start, while Israel gives diplomacy another chance, and while Sharon threatens, 'We have ways of getting the fedayeen out of Beirut.' I'm sure Sharon didn't use the word 'fedayeen' like it says in the paper, and I'm sure Sharon means what he says. No one believes me, no one wants to; I keep saying that we haven't seen anything yet, that the worst is yet to come, that a ceasefire in Beirut may not include the city as we know it, that half of it can be considered 'suburbs'. I draw little maps on pieces of paper to show them; people look at me as if I'm crazy, but I'm not. I am sure the Israelis are trying to gain time, that they will not give in until they've got what they want: the PLO. I pray to God they won't get them.

Reagan addresses another message to Begin, a 'firm' one. But will Begin listen, or is he drunk on his supposed victories? Leyla and Rasha have stopped going for their volunteer work at the College Protestant. It has received a couple of bombs, although it is French territory and is being used by the Red Cross. Israel has obviously not read the Geneva Convention and doesn't want to.

Two exits from West to East Beirut have been reopened, and some more people have left. 'Only the best have stayed, the rest is rubbish,' I say to console myself. Leyla and Rasha have found themselves two new little girlfriends, Rima and Abir. They spend their days at home playing and nagging from time to time, 'Please Mummy, take us out. Please take us somewhere. . . anywhere.' So I take them to their grand-mother's; they go to the garden and I to my vodka-orange, right in the middle of Ramadan, the Muslim month of fasting.

While we're there, I get the news: the siege of Beirut has lifted slightly and we're going to have electricity a little longer; two Israeli soldiers were wounded in an ambush; the Tunisian President has cancelled the Arab summit; the Israelis' 'patience is running out' (we're getting a little fed-up ourselves); the new US Secretary of State George Shultz would like to satisfy the Palestinians' political aspirations; Reagan is going to meet the Foreign Ministers of Syria and Saudi Arabia; and the Casino du

Liban on the Eastern side announces to all and sundry that there is no ammunitions depot in the building (we know there is).

There's yet another time-bomb to cheer us up during the ceasefire—forty-three people wounded, glass shattered for miles around. How invigorating: we had forgotten what an explosion sounded like. What's left now is the timing of the evacuation—the Palestinian evacuation, naturally, as no one is talking of an Israeli withdrawal. The Palestinians used to ask for your identity card when you approached the camps in 1975; and that's why, I am told, some Lebanese became indignant at their presence and started the war. Now the Lebanese have to bring out their identity cards for the Israelis, the Syrians, the Palestinians, the Lebanese Progressive Movement, the Lebanese Phalangists, and everybody else who's opened a 'boutique'—to say nothing of the loss of lives, the destruction, the humiliation, the exile, the loss of dignity. Satisfied? Today a new word has been added to our dictionary: 'interposition forces' that will stand between enemies (we'll need them at every corner).

As we continue to sink in refuse and the siege goes on, the Lebanese Progressives (represented by Marwan) meet with the Phalangists (represented by Amin Gemayel) to reach an understanding. Will something come of this meeting? I doubt it, and repeat that 'East is East and West is West and never the twain shall meet.'

Far away in Israel, some people are beginning to get angry at this 'meaningless' war. 'We must not enter Beirut,' says writer A.B. Yehoshua, 'it will be a catastrophe. I am pessimistic because the germs of war will remain so long as a dialogue has not been established with the Palestinians—and we know Begin has no intention of doing that.'

'This is a war without end,' says Aaron Megged. 'Each step seems justified; we're told it's a decisive step towards peace, and the result is that Israel is getting more and more deeply involved in violence and may lose itself in it.'

Jacobo Timerman, an exile from Argentina who has taken refuge in Israel, says, 'This is General Sharon's personal war, a first step towards total expulsion of the Palestinians and the installation of puppet governments in Lebanon and Jordan. I have never claimed the PLO was right, but I am sure we're wrong. The Zionist movement, thanks to Ben Gurion, chose to work politically and to reject terrorism, unlike Begin. The Palestinians must also make a choice. We must bring out this crisis, open a national debate and unmask those who wish to turn Israel into the Prussia of the Middle East.'

Many of the reservist soldiers in the Israeli army have gone back to Israel with disgust in their hearts. Avraham Burg, 27, son of the Religious Affairs Minister, has just sent a letter of protest to the people concerned to express doubts about the justice of this war.

In the meantime, General Sharon reminds us every day that the military option remains open. What is it with this man? He seems to be full of arrogance, vindictiveness and hate—what have we done to you, General Sharon?

To top it all, Iraq and Iran are at each other's throats again, to our great distress and Israel's joy. 'That should make the world forget the siege of Beirut,' an Israeli official said. Does the world know about the siege of Beirut?

Two other pieces of news today. Some people broke into the jail of West Beirut and set free 182 prisoners. One of them is an ex-neighbour of my children, a young lawyer who cut two of his guests into pieces and threw them on a rubbish dump. I hope he's outgrown these little tricks now that he's free again.

And I'm told there was a funny editorial in the French-language daily *Le Reveil* which speaks for the Phalangist Party. The editorialist, who uses the pseudonym Libanus, is very indignant. He cannot believe that French President Mitterrand could possibly make a comparison between Oradour-sur-Glane and West Beirut. How right he is. After all, in Oradour there were 'only' 2,000 inhabitants who were massacred by the Nazis; here some 500,000 people are about to be massacred by the Israelis and thousands have already paid with their lives. I begin to regret the days when I felt so unhappy that East Beirut and Zahle were being bombarded by the Syrians, Mr 'Libanus', the same people who helped you win your so-called war in 1976.

CHAPTER 10

Saturday July 17th, the forty-fourth day of Israel's war

71

against Lebanon and the Palestinians. The Tsahal (the Israeli 'Defence' Force) is everywhere but in the three square kilometres called West Beirut.

The leader of the Lebanese National Movement Walid Joumblatt has had an amazing twenty-four hours: he met with Abou Ammar in the evening, then on to President Elias Sarkis, then Ambassador Philip Habib at the US Ambassador's residence in Yarze, then on to a meeting with his opponent Bashir Gemayel, then President Hafez al-Assad of Syria, then King Hussein of Jordan. What a marathon—but who knows if anything will come of all this. I know that Philip Habib has told Walid Joumblatt 'I've been promised a flower but I'm still waiting!' Well, the vase is here and it is waiting too.

Apart from the flower, I hear that Habib is very irritated that Saad Haddad (the Israeli-backed renegade major) has taken over all the army barracks in the South. Habib protested to the State Department about this 'overkill'. Habib hasn't seen anything yet; at this point what Saad Haddad wants, Saad Haddad gets. Haddad is not the only one in the picture. There seems to be great competition between former President Camille Chamoun and Phalangist leader Bashir Gemayel: they both want the presidency. Neither has hidden his allegiance to the Israelis, but Chamoun seems to be in more of a hurry and makes daily statements that just fall short of asking for military action against Beirut. He seems to be more Israeli than the Israelis themselves.

The Palestinians meanwhile are telling anyone who'll listen that the 'Arabs are the hostages of the Israelis, not the Lebanese or Palestinians'. They are still hoping for an Arab move. The Lebanese who have stayed in West Beirut don't share this view; as far as they can see, 'they are besieged and not the Palestinians.'

Rasha is pensive today. We're at her grandmother's and the children are playing hide and seek in the bushes. Their aunt Haya and their cousin Lina are there, still refugees from the southern suburbs of Beirut. But Rasha is pensive: she has lost a tooth and she's thinking hard about whether to put it under her pillow and find it's been replaced by money the next morning, or whether she should throw it at the sun and make a wish. Suddenly, she throws the tooth into the bushes.

'What did you do that for?' I ask.

'I wanted to make a wish, but it's no use.'

'Why, what was your wish?'

'I wanted the war to end.'

I try to convince her that things are better and we'll soon all be out of this hell-hole, but nine-year-old Rasha is very sceptical and asks for specific examples. I suggest we play hide and seek, I'll hide and challenge them to find me. She forgets all about the war and I run into the garden trying to find the perfect place to hide. I find it—on the top of a tree. I clamber up and perch on a tiny branch. I hope and pray they will find me quickly; it doesn't seem such a great idea from up here. But Leyla and Rasha and their friend Abir look everywhere but up; after all, they don't expect a forty-one-year-old woman to climb up a tree. Half an hour later, I decide to take a nap and nearly fall off the branch. I giggle and the children find me; screams of laughter all around. Happiness at last! That's all I had wanted, to make my children forget for a moment what's happening in their beloved country.

I can go back to my meandering in Lebanon's political labyrinth. The meeting between Gemayel and Joumblatt is said to have been positive, the positive element being that they were photographed together. As for the rest, no one has any idea: in the picture they both look a little tense. I find out later that Bashir Gemayel told Walid Joumblatt he was running for the presidency of Lebanon and would like his approval and help in the campaign. Joumblatt's answer was negative, but he left open the possibility of future meetings. In any case, I'd like to tell them Lebanon's future seems to be out of their hands and in Begin's and Sharon's. Today Begin promises us peace, and Sharon offers temporary asylum to any unarmed Palestinians!

The Beirutis under siege look with hope to the meeting in Washington between Reagan, the Saudi Foreign Minister and the Syrian Foreign Minister. There's nearly no flour, definitely no fuel, no gas, and very little meat, which is prohibitively expensive. The situation is unbearable, but Begin should know from his own experience that no peace can be made under duress: the more you beat a human being, the less he's liable to feel the pain.

I am slightly, but only slightly, reassured by the bits and pieces we learn of Joumblatt's meeting with Philip Habib.

'Are you for the unity of Lebanon?' Joumblatt asked Habib.

'Yes, every inch of it,' came the reply.

'Don't you realise the danger in encouraging the radical right to aim for a presidential post?'

'I am for whoever the system brings,' Habib said.

'But you have become part of the system.'

In the evening of July 17th, shooting breaks out all over West Beirut. Have the Israelis finally dropped their political manoeuvring and launched their long-awaited invasion? Have some of the political factions chosen to fight it out at this awkward moment? What is it? What's going on?

'It's nothing,' someone announces, 'it's just *laylat al-qadr* [the night of destiny].' This is the night, I was told as a child, when all the trees bow down before God at midnight; if you made a wish at that hour, it would be granted. Tears come to my eyes as I remember the *laylat al-qadr* when I was fifteen and I made a wish: 'My mother is ill, I don't want her to die. Please God, don't let her die.' I had never believed in that famous night since. Tonight, twenty-six years later, in despair, anguish and anger, I make another wish: 'Please God, let me die, I simply don't want to live.'

Sunday July 18th, another day like the others. There have been two days of calm, but early this morning Tel Aviv announced that there was nothing to be gained from the Habib mission and invited the American emissary to go home. Leyla and Rasha don't want to stay home, though, so I take them to their grandmother's and come back home to work on my book. What else has happened today? Israel wants peace with Lebanon and a confederacy with Jordan. But Begin hasn't asked our opinion: he's come in like a bulldozer to the doors of Beirut to sign 'peace', leaving nothing but destruction and despair behind him. Let's hope Washington has something to say about all this and that it won't remain indifferent to human suffering.

Anyway, I'm going to try and forget all that today: I'm going to have lunch at a friend's house by the seaside. No blockade can ever be fully effective against a city by the sea. You can always drop a bomb in the water and the fish come knocking at your door. That's what our host has done, or nearly. At the lunch people exchange jokes and tell stories. The man who was responsible for organising the escape of the 182 prisoners is here. Maybe the choice of prisoners to be freed

74

should have been a little more selective? That's what I think but daren't say out loud. I would be shouted down, and anyway I'm only a woman. Most of the time women are treated like objects in the orient; men think we don't really have brains, just instinct, so they feel free to talk before us and expect us to listen.

'Please tell us about the escaped prisoners,' I ask.

'Oh, the prisoners,' the man says, 'Well, most of the guards were half drunk. There were thirty-five of us and only a few of them. When the prisoners saw us they went into a frenzy: "Please get us out of here, get us out, can't you see we're in danger here and without protection from the bombing?" We opened the gates and were nearly crushed in the rush; some were in their pyjamas, others in their slippers or barefoot. They rushed out, screaming, "God bless you, God make you strong, God. . ." and within two minutes they had all disappeared.' I am fascinated by the man's watch: I have never seen an armed element wearing such a beautiful wrist-watch before. This war is really bizarre. Some of the prisoners left for good (where did they find to stay in the three-kilometre jail West Beirut had become?), some went back to the jail and some joined different armed organisations.

The vitality of the Lebanese is amazing; nothing pulls them down for more than a moment. People are swimming in the sea outside, others are fishing, as if nothing has happened. Is it simply ignorance of the terrible situation we're in or the will to survive? I rather think the latter.

On Monday July 19th, I decide to spend the whole day with Leyla and Rasha. Their two friends join us for a little fun; we play videogames (as electricity has been generously restored except for six hours of darkness each night), scrabble, and hide and seek. I cheat at scrabble, and hide where I shouldn't, and my daughters scold me indulgently. I don't look at a single newspaper, or listen to the radio. I try to take a small nap but Leyla and Rasha's quarrelling fills the house—siblings! In the afternoon we go to their grandmother's. She has become our Mecca, and the three of us really love her. She has been paralysed for the last eighteen months and can barely talk, but she loves company. The five of us leap into the car and rush to Musseitbeh. The faces there aren't exactly welcoming.

'What's wrong?' I ask the cook. I find out soon enough:

their aunt's home has been destroyed; they've rescued a few of their things and are trying to put them into some kind of order in the garden. 'Can I help?' I ask Haya quietly. 'No thank you,' her daughter says a little brusquely. For a moment that day I had forgotten my origins; she's just reminded me. I sit on a stool and watch in frustration and helplessness. There's nothing left of their home from what I can see. I daren't ask any questions or offer my help; I'm obviously not wanted. Ten minutes later, I tell the children we're leaving and they come willingly; they've felt the hostility towards me. 'I am very sorry about what happened,' I say on the way out. 'It's not your fault, I suppose,' they say with great condescension. It's not exactly the Palestinians' fault either, but there is no use in trying to reason or use logic in times of anger; I learned that long ago.

Everyone seems nervous in West Beirut today. To my great sorrow, Nabil arrives home early this evening and announces that he intends to take Leyla and Rasha to Doha the next day. Has anything happened today I don't know about? Clearly Nabil has heard something at his uncle Saeb Salam's that has made him decide to get the children out at once.

'It's two days before the Bayram Feast,' he explains. Bayram is the Muslim feast that marks the end of Ramadan, the month of fasting. So?

'Bayram will repay Yom Kippur,' he goes on.

'Yom Kippur? You mean in the 1973 war? We didn't attack them on Yom Kippur, the Egyptians did!' The October 1973 War was fought during the Muslim month of Ramadan and launched on the Jewish day of atonement, Yom Kippur. Could Nabil really be saying the Israelis intended to begin the battle of Beirut on this anniversary in revenge? I knew politics in Lebanon made little sense these days, but this seemed to make none at all.

'It doesn't matter, they must go,' he declares.

'Go and pack,' I tell the children, 'don't worry, you'll love it. You'll be able to swim, fish, ride a motorcycle, it'll be like Camp Kiniya.' It takes them two minutes after that last sentence, which shows how much they had been enjoying the siege. Nabil is probably right, they must get out. After all, they're only children, who have seen enough destruction, heard enough bombing and witnessed enough violence for a lifetime. It is time for them to leave, but I don't know what I'll do without them. I am brought out of my thoughts by their yells: they are fighting over who takes which panties.

'Let's go and buy some more,' I say. Even with Beirut as it is, shops are following tradition and opening in the evening during Ramadan. There is no electricity so we choose the panties by flashlight.

'Why are you in such a hurry?' the shopkeeper asks.

'My children are going South tomorrow.'

'What a good idea.'

'Why?'

'They tell me that Israeli paratroops are going to be landed everywhere tomorrow.' Now where did he get his news from? He talks about political assassinations to come, reminds me of Entebbe and the commandos there, and predicts disaster. I'm beginning to think tomorrow morning will be too late. One thing is sure, people are nervous today: at Saeb Salam's, at Marwan Hamade's, at the Palestinians' headquarters.

What is it about the day's events that has raised tension to fever-pitch? I review the news in my mind:

—There's still no information about the meeting in Washington;

—Reagan has suspended the delivery of 4,000 cluster bombs to Israel;

—Ariel Sharon, after a meeting with Philip Habib, announces a settlement is possible; the only difficulty lies in the fact that no Arab country wishes to receive the Palestinian fighters—but Israel, generous as always, is willing to open its arms to them!

—Begin, on the other hand, talks of a military option (I wish they'd make up their minds together) and vows that Arafat and the PLO will be liquidated;

—The Iranians have threatened to push towards Baghdad;

—Jordan has called up its reserves;

—The President of the American University of Beirut, Mr David Dodge, has been kidnapped (I'm against all kinds of kidnapping, which I consider an act of cowardice, and I don't believe President Dodge has ever done any harm to Lebanon);

—The siege of Beirut is tighter than ever and there have been 'skirmishes' in the southern suburbs;

—The Syrians and Israelis have both reinforced their positions in the Bekaa Valley, and Syria wants to 'programme' Israel's withdrawal from Lebanon first. President Assad adds that the Syrian army has not entered Lebanon to fight Israel but to put an end to the civil war;

—There's talk about a new Kissinger step-by-step plan for the Middle East (God—not again!);

—An ammunitions dump seized by the Israelis from the PLO in the South explodes and rockets shower Galilee over a range of ten miles. The explosions are described as a 'mere accident' by the Israelis: this is some 'Operation Peace for Galilee'.

What few people know is that I received a phone call that morning from a cousin of mine in Europe who had just asked Syrian Foreign Minister Abdel-Halim Khaddam a few questions at the request of the National Movement. The answers were: yes, we will receive the PLO leaders; no, we don't wish to have ten thousand Palestinian fedayeen in our midst. The answer, which is short and to the point, takes us back to square one. Where are the Palestinians supposed to go, to Timbuctoo?

CHAPTER 11

It's 6.30 in the morning of Tuesday July 20th, and I am down in the dumps: Leyla and Rasha are leaving today for Doha. Will they make it safely? How am I going to live without them? I love them and enjoy being with them so much. I need coffee— and about half a pack of cigarettes—to pull myself together. At 6.45 I'm down in the street looking for a taxi that will take the children and Nabil, who is accompanying them, to the Museum crossing (Beirut's Mandelbaum gate). From there they'll have to go on foot, to be met by a friend of Nabil's who will take them all the way to Doha through the most unbelievably twisted road. To think it used to take barely twenty minutes to reach Doha from Beirut.

I am scared. I don't want them to be traumatised as I was in 1948, or as the Jews were in the '30s and '40s. I want them to live without hatred, but how can they? They're going to have to cross the Mandelbaum gate on foot. But then, maybe with their eternal sense of happiness they will not notice the difference and simply think it's an adventure.

Leyla and Rasha clutch their precious belongings and climb into the taxi. They wave, and I wave back with a large smile on my face. As soon as the taxi disappears into the distance I run back into their house and sob my heart out. Will I ever see them again? They are my joy, my life, the reason for my moments of happiness and anger, they occupy my time and give structure to my life. . . I don't want them to leave.

Their housekeeper, Fatima, a Moroccan who doesn't know what's hit her, comes in crying. I scold her, saying: 'What are you crying about? They're only going away for a week, for God's sake. Stop bawling and go make us some coffee.'

Half an hour later, I pick up the pieces, go home, take a bath and go out again on a more perilous mission. My aunt's cook is still living in their house on the way to the airport in a most dangerous area and keeps sending me desperate messages. The family is in Europe now but she doesn't want to leave the house with no one in it. They claim the road to the airport is filled with mines, but I go all the same. I like Rahme and I've always adored her cooking; maybe coffee with her in the garden would help me forget my children's departure. The area surrounding the house is like an ammunitions dump; rockets instead of trees line the streets, there are piles of sand everywhere, and armed elements at every corner manning cannons, Stalin's organs, and other heavy weapons. Kalashnikovs? No one even mentions those any more.

Rahme is a mass of nerves. She can't stand any more and I can understand why. If it had not been a matter of simple respect, I would have got out of there immediately and left the place and her. We sit in the garden and sip coffee gingerly while I am literally shaking inside. What if the bombers decided to go into action at this very moment? I look at her and promise to get her and her sister out of there as soon as possible. She can actually leave any time she pleases, but does not want to before she gets her employers' consent. That kind of loyalty is difficult to find these days. Back home, I spend three hours on the phone trying to get through to my aunt in France to tell her about Rahme and ask if she can leave. Finally, I get through, and as I wait for the answer we are cut off. I seethe with rage and frustration, but there is nothing more I can do about Rahme today; it will have to wait till tomorrow.

Have Leyla and Rasha made it safely? I daren't even ask the question aloud. I go to their house to see Fatima, who announces that Nabil is back. 'Where is he?' I ask, hardly believing my ears. 'At his uncle Saeb Salam's.' I take a taxi there immediately. Nabil is all smiles; the children are fine, they never noticed the crossing on foot, and they were over-joyed at the sight of the sea and the idea of swimming and fishing.

Nabil, of course, noticed the crossing and describes the humiliation. There were Israelis and Phalangists everywhere, and young Lebanese girls were befriending the Israeli soldiers; eighteen field cannons were being installed at the famous Khalde Triangle. Things are somewhat brighter in Doha, where he says the inhabitants can circulate at will, but not in the fields which have not yet been cleared of cluster bombs. Water is brought in every day by the Phalangists at the Israelis' orders; there is a curfew at 8.30 in the evening, but that shouldn't bother Leyla and Rasha.

They might not be bothered, but I am. If I thought about it in cold, clear terms, my children were safe but they were in enemy territory, in occupied lands. The people of Doha had reassured Nabil: the Israelis didn't bother them any more and stayed in their base at the entrance to the town; one could go to them for any kind of help. Great news! Am I supposed to feel happy about it? I ask him if the children noticed the planes flying over Beirut from Doha.

'No, they didn't,' he replies. 'You know Leyla and Rasha, they seem to ignore anything that could disturb their inner well-being.'

'Anyway,' I sigh, 'The Israeli air raids were only simulated.'

On the political level, Washington is insisting that the fedayeen withdraw first and the Arabs are asking for an Israeli withdrawal. The different radio stations in Beirut speculate on the talks. In Moscow, Brezhnev calls for an interposition force in Beirut and announces again that he's against US military forces in Beirut. The President of the American University of Beirut has not yet been found. One thing is sure, the Palestinians don't have him; they were furious at his kidnapping and are looking for him everywhere.

At nine o'clock this evening, katyousha rockets fall on northern Galilee. Where could they have come from? The Israelis were supposed to have 'mopped up' (another of the words in our new dictionary) the fedayeen in the area. Well, there must have been one left. . .

On Wednesday morning I wake up to the sound of the muezzin announcing the first day of the Muslim Eid al-Fitr, the Bayram Feast. Will it be 'Bayram versus Yom Kippur'? It is a good thing the children are out of this hell-hole; they've heard and seen enough. After all, the children of London were evacuated by the thousand during World War II. It's not high treason to send one's children out; it's normal procedure so long as the adults stay.

Today, for the first time in eight years, not one shot is fired to celebrate the feast; not even a child's firecracker is to be heard. Yet the children stand in the street in all their finery; the feast is a time to don new clothes and pay visits to relatives and friends. The little overdressed girls look pathetic; I suppose I don't look much better in my jeans and shirt and my loneliness.

Where am I to go today? I decide to go to the children's grandmother; the sight of me always makes her laugh, so why not bring some fun into her life, although there's nothing funny about today. Former Israeli Premier Yitzhak Rabin has said that the sooner there is a military invasion of West Beirut, the better for all concerned (except the Lebanese and Palestinians). General Mordechai Gur doesn't share this view: he believes that the Israelis should not be at the doors of the Lebanese capital. At the military level, five Israeli soldiers were killed in an ambush today in the Bekaa, and four were wounded in the South in an area between Tyre and Sidon.

Amidst all this turmoil, it is still the Muslim feast and traditions prevail. At noon, a delegation from the Chamber of Commerce and representatives of the industrialists' association come to pay their respects to former Premier Saeb Salam. They've come all the way from East Beirut by car. Only officials can still cross in this way; everyone else has to go on foot. Not these gentlemen; obviously.

'How are you Saeb Bey? We've missed you. Do tell us, how do things stand now? Will it soon be over?' they query.

'You know,' says Saeb Salam, 'it cannot be solved in a day or two. Patience is the motto of the day, patience and reason.' They nod their heads in unison. Suddenly they all sit up. The door opens abruptly and Abou Ammar walks in to pay his respects. The gentlemen's eyes nearly pop out of their heads! Abou Ammar cheerfully shakes hands with everyone and sits down. They remain standing, bid Saeb Salam a hurried farewell and stampede out of the house, back to safety in the East.

Today, all eyes are still turned to Washington, where Reagan is meeting Saudi Foreign Minister Saud al-Feysal and Syrian Foreign Minister Abdel-Halim Khaddam. The results of the meeting come later that night: it has gone well and the deadlock can be broken if the Palestinians leave for Tripoli, to be followed by disarming all of Beirut, and an Arab summit that will bring about a reasonable arrangement for better Lebanese-Palestinian relations. No armed Palestinian presence should remain on Lebanese soil, and no foreign presence, which I suppose means both Israeli and Syrian withdrawal.

Friends and relatives call me from abroad to congratulate us on the end of the war, but I think they're going a little too fast, aren't they? My cousin Ghada in London starts packing to come home. I look at all this exuberance with some cynicism, but in spite of myself I go along with it and hope for the best.

Thursday July 22nd—and I remember with a start that today is my father's birthday. He will kill me if I don't call him, but there have been no phone links with the outside world for some days unless people call us. Today I notice for the first time a small lemon tree on the balcony outside my window. It is very small but very green. There is a kind of pathetic courage about the way it holds itself up and dares to flourish in a country where so much has been scorched. It reminds me of all the green fields that still exist in the world. Will Lebanon ever be green again? Has the cancer devouring the country spread too far or can it be cured without amputation? I christen the lemon tree 'Armand'.

At two o'clock this afternoon, I decide that Ghada can start unpacking again. The Israeli bombers have returned to their ballet in the sky and this time there's nothing simulated about the air raids. They send us quite a few gifts for the second day of Bayram. It's a lovely sight: bonfires everywhere, thick, heavy smoke, nerve-shattering explosions; ninety minutes of it. After several hours of trying, I get through to my father in the evening.

'When can I come back?' he asks quietly. I feel sorry for him. What can I tell him? I just wish him a happy birthday and reassure him about the situation and, to change the subject, add the latest.

'By the way, we're eating your watermelons in Beirut,'
I say.

'My watermelons?' he says, 'You know something, the last
time we picked the watermelons in Palestine in 1947 we had
130 truckloads of them. Isn't that fantastic?'

'Yeah, sure. Well, your 130 truckloads have just reached
Beirut.'

CHAPTER 12

The fiftieth day of the war brings something a little different:
I am invited to a civilised lunch at Marilyse Izzedine's. She is a
lovely woman who works very hard for the Red Cross and still
lives in her apartment by the sea, right opposite the Israeli
vessels. If she has time for a civilised lunch, then so do I. I even
make an effort, go to the hairdresser's, put on a green silk shirt
over my jeans, and wear high-heeled sandals!

The atmosphere is cordial at her place, but the discussion
still centres on the war and the stories are quite horrendous.
One of the guests has just witnessed the cold-blooded assassination of one Khodr Muhammad Habanjar. After the assassins had
shot a few rounds into the man, they calmly came back, looked
at him, discovered he was still breathing, and benevolently put
an end to his misery.

Another of the guests, Rima Shehade, told us how she and
her husband had been protecting themselves during the
bombardments. They had built a small room in the garden out
of eighty sandbags and went in there every time the bombing
began. One day the journalist David Hirst decided to pay them
a visit, looked at the arrangement sceptically, and quietly
described to them the effect a cluster bomb would have on
such a 'bunker'.

'You should have let them be,' I say to David, who was at
the lunch.

'I know,' he answers regretfully.

At this moment, far away in his southern village of Kfar
Remmane, Deputy Abdel-Latif Zein is being arrested by the
Israelis using Saad Haddad's men. They come to pick him up
in three tanks, no less, for a 'small' interview that lasts thirteen
hours.

Things are not much better on the Eastern side. George Achkar, former head of the Broummana municipality and owner of the Printania Hotel, where many rich Lebanese Muslims have taken refuge after their flight from West Beirut, has disappeared in mysterious circumstances on his way back from Damascus. No one knows what has become of him, and late that evening people are still searching.

After lunch I go back home, and wander out on to the balcony to visit Armand, my lemon tree. Suddenly the air is filled with the sounds of explosions. Throughout lunch the bombers' dance in the sky had not stopped, but now a new element has been introduced. I can hear both the launching of nearby rockets and their explosion. Bullets whiz past my lemon tree; explosions follow one another like a lit packet of fire-crackers. I don't know whether to move into another room or not.

It's a good thing my friend Irene left this morning for New York (via Damascus) with her little daughter Miriam or she would have died of fright. Irene has gone, but she has left me with a certain responsibility—her father, whom I affectionately call the Capitaine. There is someone at his apartment to look after his daily needs, but I have promised to visit him whenever I can. He is old and paralysed and it is difficult to understand him when he speaks. All he is worried about is the electricity bill: he is convinced his electricity has been cut off because he hasn't paid it, and it's no use trying to explain to him that there are no bill collectors at the moment.

Irene must have reached Damascus by now, and so has Philip Habib. He has had seven hours of discussions there and is now on his way to Riyadh. And the Security Council met for fifteen minutes today to discuss the Lebanese crisis, a whole fifteen minutes.

As I stand in shock at the loudness of the explosions, I hear another noise on the other side of the building; it sounds like screams, or chanting of some kind. I leave Armand to his fate and run over to another balcony. About two hundred people are walking down the street, oblivious of the faction fighting in the next one. At first I can't make out what they're saying, but it's something about Sharon. Now I get it. The chant goes like this: 'Even Sharon, but not Maron (ie the Maronite)'. Hatred of the Maronites surpasses that of the Israelis: this is great for a country that's supposedly trying to reunite. Armand shouldn't see this: he would wither away discouraged!

I go back to my lemon tree and try to console him by telling him about the sixty Israeli soldiers who were hit yesterday at a barracks in Sidon, taken by surprise while they slept. Eleven of them died and twenty thousand Sidonites have been stopped and searched. The Israelis say they didn't come to stay, but they have taken over the army barracks in the South, the administrative offices, schools and some hospitals.

In the Lebanese mountain town of Aley, Bashir Gemayel meets some local Druze leaders: Emir Majid Arslan, his son Feysal, and a minister without portfolio. We watch it all on television: there's a lot of kissing and laughter, cheery smiles and great stress on Christian-Druze unity in the region. The television cameras for the most part steer clear of Emir Majid, who talks of more comprehensive unity between the Lebanese; no one present seems to want the opinion of that old but respected man.

Saturday, July 26th—some 'Shabat Shalom'. The air raids began very early this morning. I remember Begin refused to ride in a car and walked all the way to Sadat's funeral because it was a Saturday. How come pilots can get into their fighter planes on that day?

The bombers come and go at their leisure; who's to stop them? I lie in bed smoking a cigarette. Miracle of miracles, my phone has been repaired. I pick it up, listen to the tone, and hang up again: there's no one to call. Nearly everybody has gone, all my friends, my acquaintances, the people I used to work with. Well, I can always talk to Armand. I tell him about the extraordinary meeting of the Lebanese cabinet that has been called today. It's due to meet at eleven o'clock in the morning. Why so late? Some of the ministers like to sleep late, and what's the hurry anyway; only Israelis hold meetings at eight o'clock.

Some of the ministers are at such opposite poles of the political spectrum it seems useless for them to sit at the same table. When President Sarkis proposes sending a note of protest to the United Nations about the Israeli treatment of the South and its people, the pro-Phalangist Minister Selim Jahel insists on adding the words 'Palestinians and Syrians'. I wonder where Selim Jahel has been all this time: doesn't he know that there are few Palestinians and no more Syrians left in the South? A lot of shouting follows this ministerial intervention. The President's gavel is of no use. The Prime Minister gets up in anger, slams his hand on the table, nearly breaking it, and literally orders Minister Jahel to shut up. In the end the government decides unanimously to send the protest note.

As far as I can see, the meeting between Bashir Gemayel and the Druze in Aley has really been fruitful: fierce fighting has broken out between the Druze and Christians in that mountain town. It is stopped only after Israel intervenes. What has become of this country, for God's sake? The stories we hear are awful.

At an Israeli barricade, a women tells the soldier, 'Don't be afraid! I am a Christian.' She shows him the cross she wears around her neck to prove it. He angrily snatches it away and throws it to the ground as she stands there mesmerised.

In the South, some of the villagers go to Saad Haddad for help. They need water; they want Lebanese unity. They beg, argue and explain their miserable situation. He nods his head, makes no comment and suggests that some of them should come with him in his jeep without his driver. That is when he starts talking: 'You fools, do you really think I can do anything? Do you really think I am my own master? I wish I could pack up and leave right now. You poor sods, I'm more desperate than you are!'

Yet another piece of sad news is the discovery of George Achkar's corpse. I wonder how the Muslims who have taken refuge in his hotel feel.

Today is the day when parliament opens its doors for the presidential elections. A new President must be elected within the next two months. There is only one candidate so far, Bashir Gemayel, whose candidacy is announced by the Phalangist Radio this evening. Gemayel also takes the opportunity to answer questions on a programme called 'The People's Parliament'.

No matter how much of a shambles this country has become because of us and the people around us—it is still a democratic state, as I'm sure Bashir Gemayel will agree. So I'd like to participate in your 'People's Parliament' programme, Shaikh Bashir, and address these thoughts to you:

Shaikh Bashir, I knew you as a little boy when you played at your home in Bikfaya. I was a friend of your sister. Four of us formed a group then: your sister Arze, Frida, Mouna and I, a Maronite, a Protestant, a Greek Orthodox and a Sunni. We never discussed politics, nor did we ever mention our respective faiths. We didn't care. We loved Lebanon as much as we do today. I was there when Arze took her holy vows and became Sister Marie-Pierre. The last time we all met was on February 12th, 1975. . . I still remember it as if it were yesterday.

I still remember how Arze sent her parents to represent her at my graduation in 1962 because she herself couldn't leave the convent. I still remember the little Bible she sent me as a present with the following dedication: 'God is love. God keep you and protect us all', signed 'Arze, June 1962'.

But whether I am a friend of your sister or not makes no difference. Since this is a democracy, I have decided to have my own imaginary dialogue with you. I was not born in Lebanon, Shaikh Bashir, nor was I born in Palestine; I was simply born somewhere in the world. If I remember rightly your father, Shaikh Pierre, was not born in Lebanon either. It's not where you are born that matters, it is where you live and where your allegiance lies that makes you a citizen of any country. So let me tell you what I thought of some of your answers tonight.

Threats cannot be used to reassure those citizens who do not live in your 'conscription'. The threatening tone in your voice when you referred to any possible delay in presidential elections disturbed me. You talked of how Shaikh Pierre went to Parliament six years ago to elect a new president and how this is democracy. You and I and the rest of the people who stayed in Lebanon then know how those elections took place: under 'Saiqa' protection [the pro-Syrian Palestinian group], and on the understanding that no group would work to stop them. I saw the trucks which came to pick up the members of parliament at the Bristol Hotel. I saw no democracy in the presidential elections of 1976. Let's hope the democracy you talk about will be reborn before September 23rd this year, but I doubt it, as I am sure we will still be under occupation then. The Palestinians may leave, the Syrians too, but the Israelis are here to stay for a while.

You know it and I know it.

You told us that you and the Phalangists did not need anybody to free Damour, but you forget that it is the Israelis who entered Damour, cleared it and then gave the signal for the Phalangists to return. You talked of cordial Christian-Muslim relations. You will have to work very hard to make many of the Muslims forget Black Saturday. I am sure you haven't forgotten you little daughter Maya's death—I thought that was awful when she was killed a couple of years ago, but it was just as horrible as little Jehane's death [granddaughter of former Lebanese president Suleiman Franjiye] and of all the innocent children who have been killed without knowing why.

Shaikh Bashir, we need a new generation built on love to remake Lebanon, a generation that was like the group Arze, Frida, Mouna and I formed, not a group made up of armed elements who hate each other's guts. At this point East is East and West is West. We will all need time to forget the suffering and misery we have been through in the last eight years. Threats will not heal our wounds; democracy has never been built on threats.

Sidon is still under siege by the Israelis. We hear that no one can enter or leave and that people are being arrested by the hundreds after an attack on the Israeli barracks. An Israeli Phantom jet was shot down over the Bekaa tonight, as well as two tele-guided reconnaissance aircraft, by the Syrians' Soviet-made missiles. This time they used Sam-8 missiles; I have never heard of this type before. One Israeli pilot was killed and the other captured—God help us tomorrow! We have already had part of our punishment tonight: the electricity has been completely cut off.

Tomorrow is here; it's Sunday, bloody Sunday. The air raids have not stopped all day and, if I am not mistaken, have continued into the evening for the first time. In spite of the incredible thunder the bombers make, I still go out on my rounds, which now include a visit to Fatima at the children's house and one to Irene's father, the Capitaine.

Reaction to Bashir Gemayel's announcement has been mixed. Raymond Eddé calls from Paris and speaks in code: 'The position will either go to the old man who has children or to the one who doesn't.' This is quickly deciphered here to mean either Camille Chamoun or former President Charles Helou—some code! Muslim leaders are not exactly enthusiastic over yesterday's news. The Sunni Mufti (religious leader) is against holding presidential elections under occupation.

Walid Joumblatt, head of the Lebanese National Movement, calls Bashir Gemayel's announcement 'one of defiance—it is the candidacy of the Israeli tanks and cannons.' He sees Gemayel as the candidate of hegemony, partition, the single party, abolition of freedom, a peace treaty with Israel, and the end of the Arab and Islamic identity of Lebanon. Former premier Selim Hoss says no man who has fought in the civil war should be the candidate for Lebanon's highest post. Other reactions will probably come today; some people are doubtless waiting to see how low the pendulum will drop before it swings.

I've found out what a Sam-8 missile is in case anyone is interested: it is 3.2 metres long, tele-guided, with a range of sixteen kilometres; it is more mobile than the Sam-6 missiles. To me, these are no more than words on a page. I wish everybody would leave us alone and go home. Only Arafat can't really go home—that would be rather tedious for the Israelis. It has been fifty-three days, the longest Arab-Israeli war, and if the Israelis think they are winning they are mistaken. As former premier Rabin put it, Begin has got so high up a tree he doesn't know how to come down any more. Personally, I'm down in the dumps: I miss my children, their laughter, their blasé attitude to the war, our games of hide and seek.

The Israelis have eased their punishment a little: the electricity was switched back on at 9.50 this morning. And would you believe that 185 tons of flour were allowed to pass into West Beirut? But no diesel, powdered milk, oil, or medicines. How can you bake bread without diesel for the ovens? There isn't much wood in West Beirut.

I am invited to dinner tonight—the West Beirutis still find ways to pass the time! A friend who has just come down from the Chouf tells us how the Lebanese Forces have taken over the army barracks in Beiteddine, Deir al-Qamar, and Maaser Beiteddine, and how the Phalangists have taken every young Christian in every village for military training for the militia of the future. A militia against whom, since Bashir Gemayel claims he wants unity amongst the Lebanese and departure of all foreign forces?

Some people say that, if the elections cannot take place, Bashir Gemayel plans to go up to the Lebanese 'White House' in Baabda, have himself appointed President of the Council by Sarkis and take over. This is very reassuring! Meanwhile, Shaikh Bashir has long since set up a court of justice, called the 'Court of Affiliations'. Those caught in his territory who have been affiliated to one of his enemy groups in one way or another are immediately put on trial. Some get two years' imprisonment because they sympathised with Fateh for two months. Others are tried and executed for their Communist ties; twenty-seven were executed in Bhamdoun today for this very reason. Is that how Bashir Gemayel plans to rule?

Nabil is back today from a week-end in Doha with the children. Leyla and Rasha both said, when they saw him, 'I hope you're not coming to take us back to Beirut.' They may miss us, but not as much as they miss a sense of security. When the air raids are heavy over West Beirut, Rasha runs up to the roof, looks at the heavy smoke, the black clouds that cover the capital, and goes back to her frisbee without a comment. Does she think of me or does she simply suppress her feelings? I don't know but, like a child, I irrationally feel a little hurt.

It is a good thing they are not here, anyway. The air raids are definitely heavier, and the shelling by land and sea has increased. I went to see the Capitaine today, who is still insisting on paying his electricity bill. I tried to explain about the Israeli concept of punishment but to no avail.

Tuesday July 27th, and it is calm enough this morning. It seems that I slept through one hell of an air raid that lasted from 9.30 to 11.00 last night, with flares lighting up West Beirut and all; I'm glad I did.

Yesterday Arafat signed a document he gave to Congressman McCloskey (a good friend of the Secretary of State) in which he recognised all resolutions and recommendations adopted by the United Nations on the Palestinian question (which would automatically mean recognition of Israel). Israel rejected it immediately; the Americans were a little sceptical. Did this document include Security Council resolutions 242 and 338? It did, answered Arafat.

But today we have more pressing problems in West Beirut.

The air raids have become all-inclusive, touching parts of Beirut that were only lightly hit before, all around the American University of Beirut (but not the AUB itself). The heart of Ras Beirut was hit at 1.45 this afternoon, including a street parallel to Hamra Street, buildings near the Saudi Embassy, and some near the Scotch Club, a restaurant on Raouche overlooking the landmark Pigeon's Rock. The bombers come and go, like villainous visitors from outer space. Israeli pilots are assassins; if only they could look at the results of their bombings. I wish their children were here, they could have a taste of it too.

We have been punished again and have had no electricity for the last twenty-four hours. A children's song keeps going through my mind but with different words:

> *Dansons le capucine*
> *Y'a pas de courant chez nous*
> *Y'en a chez la voisine*
> *Mais ce n'est pas pour nous*

(Let us dance the capucine, there's no power in our house; there's some at the neighbours, but there's none for us.)

It is very strange to stand on your balcony and to watch the lights of Ashrafiye in East Beirut winking maliciously at the darkness that is West Beirut. I decide to call my cousin Ghada who is now in Monte Carlo to take my mind off the bombing. She is having lunch on the beach.

'What are you eating?' I ask.

'Only chicken,' poor Ghada says timidly. I laugh wholeheartedly; it is my first laugh of the day and I like the sound of it.

Three buildings in Ras Beirut have been completely flattened by the raids. We all run around looking for our friends, checking to see if everyone we know is all right. A family we know who lives in one of the badly damaged buildings has been wounded but only slightly—mother, father and three children. They look completely dazed by what has happened. As far as we know so far, eighty-eight people have been killed. I am nervous and tense, like everyone else; I still don't intend to leave, but wish better days were here so I could.

By eight o'clock in the evening, the casualty toll has mounted to 576 dead and wounded, and still the bombing continues. Maybe Begin is trying to fulfil Ezer Weizman's dream:

> We were standing on the top of a high hill, with Tyre below us. It looked deserted and shattered after months of battering by artillery and airplanes. A long snake of black asphalt caught my attention. 'That's the Beirut road!' I recalled. Memories of my youth came flooding back to me. That was the route we used to take for our weekends in Beirut. . . We had learned from experience that combat in built-up areas is always difficult, with many casualties. It was pointed out that the Syrian Army—inactive until now—would feel compelled to respond to our occupation of the city. I dropped the idea. (pp 277–278)

It looks like Begin took up that idea, and went on through Tyre all the way to Beirut.

At night the bombing becomes ferocious, and it has extended from West to East. There is still no electricity. I decide to try to light a gas lamp. God made light and fire—the lamp is on fire and so are my trousers. I scream; I am alone at home. I throw the lamp on the ground, the glass shattering around me. Water, water, and I am drenched, so is the flat's entrance. I sit on the doorstep with my head in my hands and listen to the 'whoosh' of the gas coming out of the lamp. I am no expert at gas lamps, so I plan to sit and wait for all the gas to come out. No more gas lamps for me; candles will do.

I have a huge candle in the shape of an apple, a present from a friend, May Makarem, on my birthday last year. God bless you, May, wherever you are. I think of you and the happier days when we played canasta, screamed with laughter, cursed and ate grilled meat: and we thought those were the bad days. I've heard you are stuck in the mountains in Ras al-Metn without water or electricity. I wonder if you know your fourth-floor flat in Beirut has suddenly moved to the ground floor. . . I've heard you barely have anything to eat up there, but I know you'll make it because you have courage. I hope we will both make it so we can play canasta together again like the good old days.

92

CHAPTER 13

It is Wednesday today—or is it Thursday? Let's see: if there is a cabinet meeting, it must be Wednesday, which is the regular day for a meeting. There is none, so it must be Thursday. However, I have forgotten that the Lebanese aren't like the Israelis, who meet promptly at eight o'clock every Sunday morning. The Lebanese meet at random and mainly to get at each others' throats. Today is in fact Wednesday, but there's no meeting.

Still, people from all factions are getting together, and talking to others. Philip Habib, who has gone to Damascus, Saudi Arabia, Rome, and London, lands back in Jounieh and makes his way to Baabda for a meeting with President Sarkis and Premier Wazzan. Lebanese Foreign Minister Fuad Boutros is on his way to Taef, along with the Minister of Social Affairs Abdel-Rahman Labban, who is a Muslim West Beiruti. (Good! He'll be able to describe the situation in West Beirut at first hand.)

The different political headquarters are all very busy. There's Baabda of course, but that doesn't mean much to West Beirutis, who no longer seem to be citizens of Lebanon. Our headquarters are at former premier Saeb Salam's house, which is constantly full; there's also the Ministry of Tourism, which is just as full; and the Palestinian headquarters, which changes place every hour on the hour—and how wise they are!

Today two ministers visiting the Ministry of Tourism have come 'all the way' from the East, Minister of Education René Moawad and Minister of Information Michel Eddé. Eddé is not exactly welcomed with open arms. He is a great advocate of Bashir Gemayel's candidacy at a time when the West Beirutis are becoming more and more strongly against it. Voices are raised and the discussion is becoming heated when a tall, thin figure appears on the scene: Walid Joumblatt, who is not going to be overjoyed when he sees Michel Eddé. He's not, and walks off with René Moawad while Eddé stays with Marwan to sing the praises of Bashir Gemayel to all and sundry. People start leaving, one by one, as he talks. Eddé assures us that Shaikh Bashir will be Lebanon's next president. A few months ago Eddé, as well as 107 other Maronites, had wanted to run for the presidency. What has happened to his hopes and dreams and theirs? Does he truly believe Shaikh Bashir would make a better president or is he simply under Gemayel's thumb? I know that another minister, Michel Murr, is organising the financial side of 'Operation Bashir for President'; perhaps Eddé's role is to convince people of its importance. But those who are convinced already believe it, and those who aren't will never be. He doesn't seem to realise this.

'What if I told you he has Saudi support?' Eddé says.

'Well, then let the Saudi Members of Parliament come and elect him,' is the reply. Michel Eddé looks embarrassed, but not too much.

'What if I told you he has Palestinian support?' he persists. At this moment Hani al-Hassan, Arafat's political advisor, enters the room. Michel Eddé looks flustered and stutters. What happened to his declaration about Palestinian and Saudi support? He makes no attempt to ask Hani al-Hassan, who has the answer to both. But then I wonder if Michel Eddé might not be right after all. Former Premier Salam, who is increasingly in the limelight, also knows the Saudi view. Salam is the most senior Muslim leader; he's lived it all and knows it all. He talks to King Fahd of Saudi Arabia later in the day and opposes Bashir Gemayel's candidacy: 'We the Muslims will never accept such a president,' Salam declares. 'You choose a candidate for us, we'll decide whether we want him or not. . . our candidate is "Lebanon" and nothing else.'

He also talks to President Mubarak of Egypt to convey the same message and to give him a description of the situation in West Beirut.

While everybody is talking to everybody else, Prime Minister Chafic Wazzan calls Marwan from Baabda and asks him to negotiate a ceasefire with the Palestinians. I do a quick count: this would be the seventh ceasefire. In 1975–76 there were over two hundred ceasefires during the civil war, so we still have a long way to go!

'Look for Hani al-Hassan; find me Abou Ammar; get me all the members of the Lebanese National Movement; the Prime Minister is on his way,' Marwan fires orders at his secretary like bullets. The sooner there is a ceasefire, the less the number of dead. People bustle about. It's hot and sticky and tempers flare. The ceasefire is set for nine o'clock in the evening.

We start counting: 'Ten more minutes. . . nine more

minutes. . . eight more minutes. . .' as though it were the launching of a spaceship. It's nine o'clock sharp—and the bombing is still going strong. At 9.30 we can barely hear each other speak because of the noise of the explosions. 'Oh, I forgot to tell you,' someone says, 'the ceasefire has been postponed until 10.30.' By 10.30 I'm back home and in bed. I take five milligrams of valium, leave my candle-apple on and go to sleep, only to be awakened at midnight by the loudest explosion yet. It is close but my great sense of military logistics tells me it is not too close, so I sleep peacefully on till 7.30 the next morning.

At eight o'clock I am dressed and ready for my daily tour. First, the Capitaine, who is slowly slipping. I know he is old, and I know it is time for him to go, yet sadness fills my heart. What am I going to do if he dies before Irene comes back? I like the man and I don't want him to die, damn it; what a mess. Now that Leyla and Rasha are away, my morning visit to him gives me a reason for getting out of the house.

Today is the first day of quiet after five days of hell on earth. I decide to take Fatima a small surprise of *manakeesh* (hot bread and thyme) and queue at the bakery until my turn comes. Yesterday she reminded me of the days when I arrived arms laden with *manakeesh* every morning. I take the bread and walk towards the children's house, saying good morning to nearly everyone on the way; all the faces have become familiar during the siege.

'Glad you're still alive,' says the shopkeeper.

'Thank you, I'm glad you are too.'

'Thank God you are safe,' says another.

'I'm happy to see you're all right.' These are our daily greetings now. I smile and say hello until I near the children's place, look up and stand stock-still in horror and amazement. The first two floors of the next building are flat on the ground; the debris has spilled out into the middle of the street. I start running to the house to see if everyone we know is all right. Fatima is slightly wounded; Nabil is in a state of shock; the neighbours are white-faced. The baby—what's happened to baby Saria? She is fine, just slightly wounded. There were no serious casualties, but glass carpets the floors and the doors are off their hinges. There were no armed elements at all in that building, just old West Beirutis. Still, they received fifty kilo-

95

grammes of TNT.

After two hours I manage to get Fatima off to sleep. Nabil goes off to his uncle's, while I stay behind to guard the house and read the newspapers. Washington says it is getting harder and harder to hold back Begin. If this is what it's like when they are holding him back, what's going to happen to us if he breaks loose? God preserve us! Philip Habib has twenty-four hours to get a departure agreement from the Palestinians. Sarkis and Wazzan are opposed to a Palestinian presence in either the Bekaa or the North, but Jordan, Syria and Egypt may take them in. Nobody mentions the Israelis; people seem to have gone berserk from the bombing. Another 19 were killed yesterday and 210 wounded.

But does the world care? I remember when Americans were demonstrating against the war in Vietnam; that was because of their own involvement. This time, the American administration is involved, but by proxy. Still, some Americans are upset, like those who sent letters to *Time* magazine (July 19) protesting at the horrors in Lebanon and denouncing the massive American support for Israel in the form of weapons and financial aid.

Meanwhile, Reagan assures us that there is no time limit to the negotiations (maybe we'll be able to sleep peacefully tonight), but Begin's comments to Congressman McCloskey don't sound in the least reassuring. He said: Israel has the right to destroy Beirut even if it kills ten Lebanese and five Palestinian civilians for each Palestinian soldier. Begin certainly hasn't changed since the days of the King David Hotel.* And there's a news item in the papers this morning I find hilarious: Begin has decreed El Al will no longer fly on Shabat Shalom as of September 1st in accordance with the agreement between his Likud Party and Israeli orthodox religious leaders. This does not, of course, include the bombers flying over Beirut on Saturdays, those American-made F-15s and F-16s.

To top off the morning's news, the Phalangists are protesting about the presence of '785 activists' in West Beirut that they claim belong to 'Carlos, Baader-Meinhof, the Red Brigades,

*On July 22nd, 1946, the King David Hotel in Jerusalem, the headquarters of the British administration in Palestine, was blown up by Menahem Begin's Irgun Zvi Leumi terrorist group killing eighty-three British, Arab and Jewish officials inside and five passers-by.

the Red Army, the Tupamaros' and whatnot. They still have not protested once about the Israeli invasion and occupation of most of Lebanon, which must serve their purpose at this point. What short memories they have: the Syrians once entered at their behest.

Some people do sympathise with us, though. Egyptian artists meeting in Cairo have issued a statement that they will neither forget nor forgive what Israel is doing to the Lebanese and Palestinians. And three women are sitting in the grounds facing the White House: they have been on hunger strike since yesterday. They are Nouha Hegelan (wife of the Saudi Ambassador to Washington), Hala Maksoud (wife of the Arab League Ambassador to the United Nations) and Hazar Jouejati (wife of the Syrian Ambassador to Washington). Nouha, Hala and Hazar, I greet you from West Beirut and tell you we have no need for water or electricity; what we do need is more people like you.

Fatima is feeling better, but the Capitaine seems to have reached the end of the line. I search frantically for a doctor to take with me. The doctor, a wonderfully patient man, tells me the old capitaine's ship has run out of fuel. I sit by his side until noon, and go off to yet another lunch at Marilyse's. It is not as civilised as the last one, since there is no electricity, no ice and no air-conditioning. All the doors are open to let in what breeze there is, and I can hear the waves. I close my eyes and try for a moment to imagine that I am far away on an island I always wanted to visit—Bora-Bora. I am quickly brought back to reality by the shouting in the living-room. The Minister of Information is here and he is shouting loudest in response to the criticism of some of the people present.

'No one, but no one, can give me lessons in patriotism,' he yells, 'I am for legality.'

The favourite topic of conversation today is Bashir Gemayel's candidacy. Diatribes follow in quick succession about the chamber of deputies, the legal aspects of quorum, the constitution, what happened a hundred years ago, what is going to happen in a hundred years' time. . . no one has any answers about what's going to happen today, though. Once again, being a woman in our country I can listen but not talk, so I listen.

I hear that Camille Chamoun has not forgotten what happened to his son's forces two years ago and that he conducted himself with decency when he went to his old home town of Deir al-Qamar in the Chouf: he simply visited his wife's grave, went around the village, sent a message of thanks to the National Movement for having kept everything intact, and discreetly went home. Camille Chamoun is an old fox and a politician.

I also hear René Moawad, the Minister of Education, saying that schools will not reopen soon. Even schools in the East have been occupied by the Israelis, and he doesn't know what to do. I am already thinking about what to do with Leyla and Rasha if schools don't start again in October.

As soon as lunch is over I walk on to the balcony to look for the Israeli gunboats. I can't see them, but I can hear something.

'What's that?'

'It's the gunboats,' says Marilyse, our military expert for the day.

'What are they doing?' There was supposed to have been a ceasefire.

'Fishing, maybe?'

I try to remain cool and collected. There have only been four explosions today so far, and let's not forget that ceasefire. . . At 4.45 in the afternoon the ceasefire is over. The Israelis say we breached it: Israeli gunboats were only trying to stage a landing, what was wrong with that? Did we have to shoot back at them for such a simple thing? We get the whole works for being so presumptuous as to try to stop them landing: air raids, gunboats, shelling from land artillery; neighbourhoods are on fire, cluster bombs explode everywhere.

René Moawad, who has gone home to the East, calls Marwan and asks frantically:

'What's happening?'

'I don't know. Where is Philip Habib? Isn't he going to do anything? This is genocide, pure and simple.'

As they try to arrange yet another ceasefire, I sit and chat to a top Red Cross official who tells me how he just managed to get eighty thousand pounds of medicine into West Beirut. They were a gift from the United States, and the Israelis did not even allow the Americans to bring them in, so he's proud of his achievement. I wish the Americans would send us less medicine and the Israelis fewer weapons.

I learn a lot of interesting things while I sit there waiting for the bombing to end. The Israelis are definitely as corrupt as anyone else. One man tells the story of how some of their soldiers were willing to let in eight barrels of diesel in exchange for one kilo of hashish. A man crossed from East to West in his car, almost a miracle these days. He explains how he handled the Israeli checkpoint: he cut a $100 bill in two, gave the soldier in charge half the bill, and promised him the rest on his way back.

In the evening, we hear that the captured Israeli pilot, now in Beirut, is nervous and edgy. 'I am forty-six and in the reserves. . . I've been a pilot for twenty years. . . I've been in all the wars, bombed every place. . . this is the first time I have been bombed myself. . . it's awful,' he says as the walls shake around him.

Voice of Israel Radio gives a cool breakdown of what is happening to us; the Phalangist Radio goes into even more detail about how we are being battered. I switch back to the Voice of Israel—it sounds more objective at this point and that's saying a lot.

Everybody is exhausted and tense; what the hell is happening? I don't know and there's nothing I can do. I am going to go home and take a valium: at least I'll die dreaming of Bora-Bora.

Walid Joumblatt met Philip Habib the next morning and told him that from now on we all had a spokesman—former premier Saeb Salam—'he speaks for all of us.' I am happy at this piece of news because I respect and admire Saeb Salam for his courage and fortitude.

It's Saturday and ceasefire number eight begins. I hope to God it lasts, we're all very, very tired. The lack of electricity and water does not help much. Some people are still trying to keep up their spirits—I got a note from Rima Shehade (the 'bunkerhaus' lady) this morning inviting me to lunch. Their house is a magnificent example of an old Lebanese home, built in 1885, and it feels good to be inside it. I can pretend I'm in the old Lebanon for a while. It's good to enter a bathroom and be able to flush the toilet and hear the water rushing down. It's good to be among people who are making an effort to sound cheerful in spite of their anguish.

Salwa al-Said, the former president of the Baalbek Festival, is here today. She lives next to a building that went crashing down two days ago. So far they've found 105 corpses in it; she tries to put up a show but she's angry at the world. She has brought the Ambassador of Canada, Mr Arcand, along with her, and we all drink a toast to him for having stayed with us. Only four other ambassadors have made this choice as far as I know: the Greek, the Yugoslav, the Soviet and the Austrian Ambassadors. The others come and go, some don't come at all, and there's just one Arab ambassador, from Yemen.

Each describes their experiences during yesterday's bombing. Tammam Salam, head of the Makassed (the Muslim benevolence organisation) tells us of the hard blow they've been dealt: the children's section at the Makassed Hospital has been badly hit; wounded children were injured again. A doctor lost both legs, but they have managed to get him out for treatment in France. He looks at our miserable faces and tries to find something to cheer us up.

'You know how we extinguished some of the fires? With sea water. So you see things aren't so bad. We'll always be able to put out fires. By the way, Rima, I've seen your bunkerhaus—it'll be great for your cat! And is that a white sheet I saw on the roof?' he said teasingly about this possible sign of surrender.

'It's not white, it's beige,' Rima answers indignantly. We all laugh at this, and I tell them the story about some people in Damascus who, during the 1967 war, washed all their white linen, put it on the roof, and watered it for days on end whenever it became too dry!

There's a big note on the wall, a white cardboard sign that says: Do not talk politics. 'Why is that there?' asks the Canadian Ambassador.

'We put it up one week after the war began. Discussions were becoming too heated and we had lost nearly all of our friends. So we decided to put it up to keep the few that were left.'

'Do you know that for the first time the Israelis used a bomb that weighed one ton yesterday?' I say. 'They dropped it on Spinney's supermarket but it didn't explode. If it had three or four buildings would have vanished into thin air. Bomb disposal experts came and took care of it. They went on their way carrying 1,000 useful kilos of TNT, a little gift from Israel!'

'Can you believe it?' someone calls out, 'The ceasefire is still holding.' We all touch wood. . .

There may be a ceasefire in Beirut, but Druze and Christians are fighting each other in Aley and other mountain towns. We don't have all the details yet, but the Phalangists seem to have started it. 'They're even searching our veiled women,' one Druze shaihk says indignantly.

August 1st, and I wake up at 3.15 in the morning. I had a nightmare: rats, snakes and cockroaches crawling all over me. I don't want to go back to sleep—I can still see the rats. Should I take a valium just because of a nightmare? I try to go to sleep while thinking of Leyla and Rasha. I miss them. . .

At 3.16 it's pitch black outside and Armand is very still. Has the little lemon tree sensed something? It's hot and sticky and I need to go to the bathroom. I don't feel like getting out of bed; it's so eerie outside. . .

At 3.17, one explosion follows another; the gunboats and field artillery have simultaneously gone into action. God, what's happening? It's suddenly light not dark, but we're a long way from dawn. The flare-bombs have gone into action too. Today, Sunday August 1st, is my cousin Ghada's birthday. It is Menahem Begin's birthday too. Along with the birthday cake in the shape of a tank, he has clearly decided to give himself an extra present. Happy Birthday, Mr Begin, from all the children of Lebanon. I hope you've decided to have a short ceremony.

By 6.07, it looks as if Begin does not want a quick party. The bombers have arrived to take part in the festivities. Sixty F-15s and F-16s give cover to air raids by the Skyhawks; they come and go in waves. I look out from the balcony: the refugees in the public garden of Sanayeh have nowhere to go for shelter. Some of the children even stand in queues to fill the family gallons at burst water pipes. A bomb a second; at $1,000 a bomb, that's quite an expensive birthday present for the sixty-nine-year-old Mr Begin.

At 7.15 the bombing is continuing. I can't see anything any more. The sky of Beirut, so blue in the summer, looks like the foggy sky of London—but we have sixty Jack the Rippers here. The planes hit at random. Hospitals, schools filled with refugees, churches, mosques, nothing is spared. Surely I read somewhere this was against the Geneva Convention.

At 7.45, I turn solemnly to Marwan to suggest going down to the shelter; things are getting a little spooky up here on the eighth floor. By 8.15 we are down on the ground floor, in the house of an old friend of Marwan's. Samia is scared, but she never loses her cool. Traditions come first and we're offered coffee and tea. Most important of all, Marwan can be next to a working phone. He calls up his brother-in-law, Ghassan Tueni, the Lebanese Ambassador at the UN. A bomb a second— it hasn't stopped, but it must; planes have to refuel sometime.

'It's a massacre,' Marwan tells Tueni, 'you must call for an urgent meeting of the Security Council.'

'At 2.15 in the morning?'

'In a few hours' time there won't be anything left to call a meeting for.'

Ambassador Tueni promises to do his best. In the meantime, another man is active: Saeb Salam. He tells Marwan that he's called New York too, and spoken to Egyptian Ambassador Ismat Abdel-Meguid, as well as Ashraf Ghorbal, the Egyptian Ambassador to Washington. Ambassador Ghorbal wakes up the State Department and talks to Secretary of State Shultz who promises to do what he can.

'I'm sure they can do something. Israeli Foreign Minister Shamir is in Washington, Shamir is in Washington.' I am beginning to sound like a stuck gramophone record! The planes are dipping lower and lower. Should we go to a shelter? Is there a shelter from this kind of storm?

'Saeb Bey, I've talked to Ghassan Tueni,' Marwan tells the former premier, 'a Council meeting is going to be held at 6.30 this morning, that's 12.30 our time.' God, that will be too late. . . we'll all be dead by then. I keep these thoughts to myself. Everyone is too scared as it is. It is the weekend in New York, after all, and it is difficult to get hold of fifteen ambassadors. I think about Fatima, about the Capitaine. I call up the children's grandmother and find out that Saeb Bey has taken refuge at her place on the ground floor, proof, if it were needed, that things are really bad. Saeb Bey rarely moves from the upper floor during bombing.

In all of Lebanon only two people are trying to put a stop to this genocide in West Beirut: Saeb Bey and Marwan. Just a few weeks ago Philip Habib told Saeb Salam he was reading the book I had written on the civil war. When I heard this I sent Saeb Salam a copy with the following dedication: 'To Saeb Bey whose courage I have always admired. May he convey a message to those concerned that people may die but causes never.'

Saeb Bey hasn't shaken my belief in him; here in West Beirut he's trying to do something for us. He calls up Philip Habib: 'What's this, Phil? What's this? You know you can do something.' He gives President Sarkis a piece of his mind. Sarkis a President? Some of the West Beirutis are now referring to him as the Nero of 1982! Can't he see what it is like here from where he is?

The 'carpet bombing' (another term we learn) continues. By three o'clock in the afternoon some 185,000 bombs have fallen on our heads, and still the party goes on. A bomb a second, many of them the type that were dropped on Spinney's but this time they explode. A ceasefire has been announced for five o'clock—will we still be alive by then? What are Leyla and Rasha thinking—they can see it all from Doha. Tears start pouring down my cheeks. 'It's nothing,' I say quickly, 'I'm just a little drunk. I'm sorry. . . What? No, no, I'm not scared.' All I've done since this morning is pray.

5.07 and there's not a sound outside. Nobody dares even breathe. We look at each other in wonder. Are we still alive? How many are still alive? Little by little the news starts filtering through. Saeb Salam's home has been hit but everyone there is all right. When he came out on his balcony at 5.10 people started shouting with joy to see him—and the tears came to his eyes.

One way or another we're all crying. Much of West Beirut is beyond repair, pulverised into the ground. I understand Ariel Sharon had a son who died piloting a plane in one of the Arab-Israeli wars. If this is true he's had his revenge—on the only Arab country that has no military planes and no pilots.

The Israelis have taken over the airport and advanced five kilometres down the southern road coming from the rubbish dump at Khalde. I am sure this will not be enough for them, and everybody else here shares this opinion. The Syrian Brigadier Muhammad Hallal, who heads their remaining forces in West Beirut, believes this too, but he has nothing more to give. He has just emerged from the debris of a building somewhere in Ramlet al-Baida (just down from the corniche at Raouche) and he can barely hear us.

Brigadier Hallal has seen the wheel turning, lived through it all. In 1973 he had his first meeting with Amir Drouri (now Commander of the Israeli forces occupying Lebanon) on the Golan Heights. He was told to retreat, his children's names were called out one by one on the loudspeaker, he was told that no one was coming to his help—yet he stayed and fought and his children waited for him patiently. In June 1976 he shelled West Beirut with a vengeance: the irony of it all; in 1982 he's fighting alongside the people of West Beirut. Today he has lost eleven men and has only eight more tanks and six cannons. He smiles and tries to joke but one can see the despair in his eyes. He knows the Israelis will try to advance again: if he tries to stop them, Tel Aviv will scream bloody murder about a breach of the ceasefire; and if he doesn't they will soon be in Ras Beirut, one of the last remaining bits of Beirut. The Palestinians and the Lebanese National Movement know this too.

There are hundreds of casualties, and no one can even begin to estimate the damage. Every single person I meet that evening has lost his or her home. Dr Samir Sabbagh went into his house to get something, came out of the door and the staircase was gone; he hadn't even heard the rocket that blew it away. Sabah Ramadan, who works at the Lebanese Radio Station, is red-eyed; he's lost everything and doesn't want to talk about it. Samira, the Capitaine's housekeeper, has lost her home but she doesn't mind as long as her family remains alive. Late that night the fires are still burning. There are no more streets, no more roads, no nothing, but everybody is kissing everybody else and offering congratulations on being alive.

Hani al-Hassan says desperately, 'We'll go, we'll leave to-morrow, but Sharon doesn't want to negotiate. He and Begin want only one thing, to annihilate us.'

'No, don't go just yet,' says one of the Lebanese leaders, 'go when everything has been destroyed and only one building is left standing. Then we'll be able to invite the American tourists into West Beirut and show them one building and a camel. You know how they always want to see camels.' He is trying to make it easier on Hani al-Hassan, to defuse the situation for all of us.

'You know, Hani,' another says seriously, 'You must go right now or else there won't be anyone left to go!' We are really a cheerful lot tonight!

This is how the day ends:

Resolution 516 (1982). Adopted by the Security Council at its 2386th meeting on 1 August 1982.

The Security Council,

Reaffirming its resolutions 508, 509, 511, 512 and 513 (they must be getting tired by now!)

Recalling its resolution 515 of 29 July 1982,

Alarmed by the continuation and intensification of military activities in and around Beirut,

Taking note of the latest massive violations of the cease-fire in and around Beirut,

1. Confirms its previous resolutions and demands an immediate ceasefire, and a cessation of all military activities within Lebanon and across the Lebanese-Israeli border;

2. Authorizes the Secretary-General to deploy immediately on the request of the Government of Lebanon, United Nations observers to monitor the situation in and around Beirut;

3. Requests the Secretary-General to report back to the Council on compliance with this resolution as soon as possible and not later than four hours from now.

I pay a special visit to Saeb Salam, 'I've come to say thank you, and tell you I have the highest respect for your courage. You're one of the few who has done anything. God bless you.' He answers, 'You're not doing too badly yourself', which gives me a bit more courage to keep up a front. Inside I am really very scared: I don't want to die. I like life in spite of all its problems; I like every single person who has stayed in West Beirut; I've made new friends, talk to everybody, enjoy our discussions, eat anything I find and sometimes forget to eat for a whole day (but never forget to drink).

Marwan says Raymond Eddé has been right all along: there is a plan to divide Lebanon into four parts. There's talk of annihilation, balkanisation, Vietnamisation—nothing about civilisation. If Marwan is right, God help us; we can't stand much more of this. Because of the increasingly alarming talk about another round, I go to visit all the neighbours in the building where I live urging everyone to co-operate in preparing the shelter.

Each day I think, where are the Arabs? During the Six-Day War in 1967, the people of Cairo painted their car lights blue and that's all they felt of the war; they left $1 billion worth of equipment behind them in Sinai. There were only eighteen dead in Jerusalem, in Nablus not one shot was fired when the Israeli army went in. Syria didn't do much better. Three regular armies were beaten almost in the first two hours of that war. Here, a vagabond army of Lebanese, Palestinians and Syrians is in its sixtieth day of war against one of the strongest enemies in the world. Oh, I'm not kidding myself; I know the Israelis are taking it easy to avoid great losses. But we did receive 215,000 bombs on our head yesterday, and that's not taking it easy, while the Israelis couldn't advance very far. Dresden, Nuremberg and Berlin together can't compare with what we went through yesterday.

The Canadian Ambassador has left West Beirut on the orders of his government. It was only the day before yesterday that we drank a toast to him. It is sad to see him go. The Austrian Ambassador has gone too; his residence was badly hit yesterday. They both went to the East. Thank you, Mr Ambassadors, anyway; you stayed with us long enough and endured more than your share.

CHAPTER 14

I haven't been able to write a single word in the last four days. I can barely tell night from day; I've hardly slept and then only with the help of valium. This book reminds me of the *Diary of Anne Frank*. She was in a small room hiding from the Nazis. I'm in a big prison unable to hide from the 'Judeo-Nazis' (Amnon Kapeliouk—*Le Monde*'s correspondent in Jerusalem—has given the Israelis this name).

I don't remember much about the last four days. I know I've wept a great deal; I know I needed to talk to my family but I couldn't get through; I know there were a few hours of quiet when I went to check if Fatima and the Capitaine were all right. I walked to their houses and saw the rats at high noon scampering merrily in the streets undeterred by human beings or noise. Children threw stones at them for fun as I watched mesmerised. I know that one evening, nearly out of my wits with fear, I ran barefoot down the stairs not knowing where to hide from the bombing. What can I write about the last four days: that several times I came within inches of death? That I am scared? That I don't want to leave? There are hundreds of thousands of Anne Franks in West Beirut today. I cried when I read her diary. Who is crying for us?

Every time the Lebanese Government is about to reach a settlement, the Israelis start bombing us from land, sea and air. The last few metres of West Beirut that were safe, the area where I live, has turned into Dante's inferno. Not one building has been spared; not one neighbourhood. I saw eight children blown to bits as they were queuing for water at the Sanayeh public gardens. I saw their legs, arms and heads flying in all directions.

I saw the wounds caused by the phosphorus bombs when I searched through the injured at the AUB hospital, hunting for an old friend of mine, Karam Hirdane. I had worked with him during the civil war trying to locate and free kidnapped people. The wounded were lined up by the hundred in the hospital's basements, some without legs, others with only one arm, the dead lying next to the living.

One day when it was quiet—at 1.55 in the afternoon—I saw two planes swoop down from the heavens right to where we were, and heard something that sounded like the cracking of a whip. There was no other sound, just the cracking of a whip: people ran up and down the streets at that terrible sound; the few cars still on the streets nearly collided; children cried and women screamed, but no one knew what had happened. We scrutinised the horizon: no dust, no fire, no noise—just the sound of the ambulance sirens. And then I noticed a space where a building had been, right behind the public gardens. Impossible—there had been no noise. I ran to the spot. An eight-storey building had disappeared. People ran around half-crazed, women screamed their children's names. A white wedding dress lay on the ground nearby.

Little Anne, I'm going to tell you about vacuum bombs. You told us about the holocaust, the gas chambers, the little children who disappeared and were never seen again, about Auschwitz, Dachau and the injustice of the world. The vacuum bomb creates a void and can obliterate a building without making a sound; it's known as an 'implosion'. It is said to be an American invention. When Philip Habib asked Ariel Sharon what the hell he had done that for, Sharon answered that this wasn't a breach of the ceasefire but a 'special commando operation'.

There were two hundred and fifty people in the building that crumbled down, innocent refugees from the South. Abou Ammar had left the building just three minutes before it was hit. I can still hear the screams of those who were still alive. Even two days later one of them had the presence of mind to turn a radio on very loud and then off, on and off, trying to signal where he was. I prayed and prayed, please God, let them come out alive, please God, they don't deserve to die. Hundreds of people tried and tried to get them out and couldn't. They're all dead now. They must have gone through hell, hoping and hoping, and then. . . death.

Anne Frank was very young when she died; I suppose I'm old enough to die. I ran from room to room, from floor to floor, playing games with death, trying to escape. But now I don't care any more. I am exhausted and so are all the little children of West Beirut. I miss my children. The phone links between Beirut and Doha are cut so I haven't talked to them. They've sent me word that they are fine. I am happy for them but God how I miss them. I miss Rasha's daily question 'How is Abou Ammar?' and Leyla's 'Have we won them yet?'

Rasha, do you know that Abou Ammar is leaving soon—alive, I hope—and Leyla, do you realise that no one ever wins anything in war, that there's only misery on both sides?

Do you know that I've washed and buried the Capitaine? That I borrowed a coffin which I had to return to the priest immediately after the burial? That I cried and cried by his side while he lay dying, not for him but because I kept hearing the screams from the flattened building close by? That one day I went to get bread for the Syrian soldiers standing guard at the Ministry of Information and when I came back four of them were dead?

And they tell me things are getting better, that there's optimism in the air.

'What will you do when they leave?'

'I'll dance in the streets?'

'When who leaves?' I asked.

'The Palestinians, of course.'

'And what will you do when the Israelis stay on?'

'They're not going to leave?'

'You mark my words.'

We hear the multinational forces are going to arrive simultaneously with the Palestinians' departure, or so Philip Habib says. No, says Begin, Palestinians out first, the multinationals in later. The French Ambassador talks of a French force arriving. Two of our acquaintances were shot to death yesterday, nobody knows why. They were hastily buried with no one to attend and without coffins. There are no longer any coffins for sale in West Beirut; you borrow and return them.

I slowly begin to fill in the gaps in those four days of horror. August 4th was the worst: it is coloured black, red and yellow in my mind. The people who took refuge in the 'safe' square that was Sanayeh have fled back to Sabra, the Palestinian refugee camp in the southern suburbs, and that's saying something. Fatima's friends, where she went to have tea each day, died in the bombing. Everything was on fire before our eyes: orphanages, schools, cinemas. The phones gave out on us too; this time Marwan was only able to get in touch with Ambassador Tueni at the UN once. For the first time in the long, long siege, no newspapers came out.

We didn't have much faith in the message President Sarkis sent to President Reagan during those days; and Premier Wazzan was in his shelter with his phones out of order. All this happened without the Israelis even claiming a breach of the ceasefire to explain their sudden offensive or the twenty-hour battle that followed. The Israelis have now moved down to the Golf Club, apart from the positions they took at the airport, but they've suffered heavy losses at both the Museum crossing point and at Beirut Port and have been unable to move forward. Shall I call it black Wednesday for mourning, red Wednesday for blood or simply yellow for cowardice? I choose yellow—hitting from afar without seeing the adversary is easy; it's like playing space invaders on a video-game and never feeling a thing.

Do you think that in all those days the Lebanese presidential candidate uttered a word of protest against this deadly, barbaric offensive? Shaikh Bashir, you know what former US Ambassador Dean Brown said about your father, Shaikh Pierre, who founded the Phalangist Party? He said: Shaikh Pierre saw the glory of Hitler's Germany in 1936; the pity is that he never went

109

back to see it in 1945.

The real pity is that we feel so confused and lost in West Beirut. The little things that help place you in your world and in your life are lost, one by one. You can't even rely on your daily paper for the date. For *L'Orient-Le Jour* (the French-language daily) August 1st became August 2nd!

Today is August 8th. I sit at a table in one of the few hotels remaining in West Beirut next to a group made up of most of the members of the Lebanese National Movement. It is Walid Joumblatt's birthday and they're trying to celebrate it as best they can. Someone cracks a feeble joke: 'I'm not staying long, just to wish you a happy birthday. I'd better get out of here before the next vacuum bomb lands as a gift.'

On August 9th, I ask what day it is and find out it's Monday. The beginning of the week but the continuation of an endless bombardment. The fighter planes have gone into action again, and there's no sleeping day or night. I am angry at everyone except those who have stayed in West Beirut.

Last Wednesday, the red, black and yellow Wednesday, was Yasser Arafat's birthday. He had tried to spend it discreetly, but the Israelis insisted on celebrating in grand style. Abou Ammar, no matter what happened on Wednesday, no matter what happens in future, I wish you a very long life because I have nothing but respect for you and the people you lead. Most of you deserved nothing but the best and you got nothing but the worst. Don't blame your enemies the Israelis—you always knew they were your enemies—blame your brothers the Arabs who were not there when you needed them.

Israel's Deputy Chief of Staff Moshe Levy was killed that Wednesday night while directing operations against West Beirut. Who said our people couldn't fight? An army of vagabonds stood up to the Tsahal, all 120,000 of them!

One day last week I managed to get a line to Washington and spoke to Nouha Hegelan who was going on with the hunger strike in front of the White House along with the wives of the other two ambassadors. 'What can we do for you?' Nouha asked. 'Nothing, you've done enough and we thank you for it,' I told her, 'nothing can stop the Israelis except the United States.' When we learned that the fasting women were nearing the end of their tether and would shortly be hospitalised, Premier Chafic Wazzan and his wife sent them the following message:

'On behalf of the inhabitants of besieged West Beirut, we salute you and all those who have joined you in your fast for the lifting of the siege of West Beirut. . . You have set an example to other people in the world and have influenced public opinion as much as you can. We beseech you to end your vigil and your hunger strike. We need you with us to build a better Lebanon.'

Another cable was sent to them signed by the 'three remaining ministers in besieged West Beirut': 'Your courageous action honours and touches us all. More suffering and misery on your part will not help lift the siege of Beirut, nor will it help stop the Israeli aggressor. However, it has made our people's suffering known to the world. You have done enough. We beg you to stop your vigil and send you our deepest thanks.'

I don't know what happened to Nouha, Hala and Hazar; the air raids are so heavy I no longer have the strength to think or run. There was supposed to have been an agreement between the Americans, Lebanese, Palestinians and Israelis: the French were coming in, the Palestinians were going out, a thousand here, a thousand there, to Jordan, Egypt, Sudan, Iraq. What has happened to Syria? Its radio constantly honours our resistance and encourages our steadfastness. The hypocrisy of this world is unbearable.

It's 5.55 in the evening and the air raids haven't stopped for a second. I am not going down to the shelter no matter what happens. The screams of the thirty people trapped in the vacuum-bombed building in Sanayeh are still fresh in my mind. I would rather die a quick death than wait and hope and slowly suffocate.

If we're being bombed so hard again, there must be a reason. There's nothing on the political level that makes any sense, so it must be somebody else's birthday. Happy birthday, Ariel Sharon, if this is your day! I hear you operate by computer in tents far away. You push a button and whoosh, the tanks fly into the sky. We don't have to watch science fiction movies when we have you. We couldn't watch anything anyway since there is no electricity; and as for the water you've so generously given us back—it's just pouring down the streets because you have destroyed the pipes.

And I hear you and Shamir and Begin aren't getting on so

111

well any more—what's happened? Can we help to bring you back together again? What's it to be now, the multinational forces first or the Palestinians? And can one of you explain the difference between the 'multinational' force and an 'international' force? Do you know that this is the sixty-sixth day of your war with little Lebanon, and not one white flag has gone up yet over our lovely destroyed capital? I'll let you into a secret: you haven't won. No one has won; we've all lost something, you more so than us. Today you tell us again you do not want to enter West Beirut. You and I know why: the Tsahal would suffer too many losses and how would you explain those to the people of Israel?

I am told by several people in 'town' that today is Wednesday. In fact it is Tuesday, as I can tell from one of the few newspapers that are still coming out in besieged West Beirut. Our best-known Arabic daily, *Al-Nahar*, and its sister paper *L'Orient-Le Jour* had to close on August 4th when a rocket blew up their offices. It was *Al-Nahar's* fiftieth anniversary that day. There's an old lady who has refused to read the papers since then. Her name is Adele and she's reading magazines instead. Throughout the siege she spent her whole day reading the *Nahar* of the day before to give herself a feeling of security. We tried giving her some of last month's copies but she was not fooled.

I don't read the papers any more either. It's not that I'm not interested, but what's the point? I have all the news right before my eyes. I've made a tour of what remains unoccupied of West Beirut, and I've seen it all. During my tour of the destruction, the desolation and the horror, I think of days gone by. I remember my sixth birthday party in Jaffa, and our house which overlooked Tel Aviv. I remember the time when I was eight years old and attending the College Protestant in Beirut. My schoolmates made fun of me because of my Palestinian accent. The way I tried to attract the teacher's attention, raising my hand and saying, 'Miss, Miss, can I read, can I read?' meant 'I am a cow, I am a cow' in the Lebanese accent. I was bright so I soon learned. It's strange, but I have a brother who was born in Nablus in March 1948, the year we left, and until today he still speaks with a Palestinian accent; God knows where he picked it up from.

I was head of my class at school and I was proud of it.

Several years later, when I was applying for a place on the UN staff council, I ran against an Israeli girl, and I got the job. I still remember her, Alicia Margolioth. I rarely spoke to her, but I never felt hate for her. Where is she today? Is she for or against the war? I understand that only nineteen per cent of the Israelis are against this genocide called 'Operation Peace for Galilee'. Someone pointed out today that the Lebanese have such short memories they'll soon be calling this the 'incidents of Summer '82' (they refer to the civil war as the 'events'). I had one turning point in my life, and I still wonder whether, if I had accepted a scholarship to study in Japan in 1967 instead of a post at the UN, I would be here today.

I am glad to be here and I am proud to have had enough guts not to have left West Beirut. I know I'm taking a big chance but, although I care very much about life, I'll stick it out because this is my mother's country, my country, and my children's country, and I love every inch of it.

Leyla and Rasha are very happy where they are in Doha; they sent me their news with Nabil. It seems they don't want to come back to Beirut and that they try to ignore every piece of bad news coming out of here. They've built up a wall of self-defence; I hope nothing makes it crumble. Leyla and Rasha are staying in the only house in Doha which doesn't have a white flag on top flying from a mast. Meanwhile, the Israelis have taken over four houses in Doha; they seem to like it there. They seem to like it everywhere in Lebanon. I heard that they even tried to take over the port of Jounieh in Phalangist-controlled territory: I found that amusing. There were other ironies too: I smiled when I heard that Menahem Begin was complaining of having 'fought alone' in Lebanon, without Phalangist help! The Phalangists may not have actively participated in the bombing and shelling of West Beirut, but they certainly aren't spreading confidence among us. It seems that two days ago they shot and killed a woman and her two little girls somewhere in South Lebanon—the Israelis and Saad Haddad's forces had to step in to punish them!

We continue to hear stories about corruption in the Tsahal. They took over the airport on Sunday and by Monday it was totally cleaned out. Even a Cessna disappeared, but I'm sure it flew off on its own—after all, we are so often assured that the

Tsahal comprises honest men raised on ideals and principles. . . Israeli General Amos told Philip Habib after the airport 'incident': 'I am ashamed to belong to such an army.' I wonder what the Israelis did with the duty-free goods? I ran out of cologne a long while back, and I stink most of the time now.

'We had a little baby boy this morning,' I told a neighbour today.

'That's great, but—I didn't know you were married.'

'I'm not. One of the refugees had a baby yesterday in the entrance of the building.'

'My God, how fantastic. What did she name him?'

'Hissar [the Arabic word for siege].'

'Who helped in the delivery—your neighbour, Dr Negib?'

'No—Abou Abed, the doorman.'

As I sit down to write, I ponder the latest news from abroad. Some people ran into a kosher restaurant in the Rue des Rosiers in Paris and shot at everyone in sight. I know nobody here was responsible since we're too busy trying to escape death ourselves, so who was? I don't like this new wave of anti-Semitism. I have always taught Leyla and Rasha that an Israeli is one thing and a Jew is a completely different matter.

The bombing is becoming very violent again. Saeb Salam calls up Philip Habib: 'Phil, what the hell is happening?' Phil replies: 'You go to your basement, and I'll get down to work.' Twelve minutes later, the savage bombing stops, and we are given a wonderful gift: a night of peace and quiet.

So much for our night of peace: the bombing has resumed from air, sea and land. It is now 11.05 at night and the Israeli planes are getting nearer all the time. Everyone keeps saying things will get better. Can they get any worse? We have been without electricity and water for twenty-one days; we get bombed every Wednesday and Sunday, with a bonus on Tuesdays and Fridays. I still haven't gone down to the basement, being a fatalist at heart; you only die when your time has come. My time seems near.

Good morning, Beirut. It's a lovely Wednesday morning and the sky is turquoise blue. A little breeze is blowing through the window and Armand looks as happy as I feel with his leaves waving gently. It's quiet outside and that's the main thing. I walk through the streets of my capital, the dirty, rat-infested streets where everyone looks bewildered, but it is my capital and I love it.

In the afternoon, I come crashing down from the morning's euphoria. I lie down on my bed to catch up on a little sleep, just in case, and the world spins every time I close my eyes. I come out of a deep faint with something being pushed under my nostrils. I don't recognise a soul around me, but I know something is happening to me and it's a terrifying feeling. The doctor Marwan has brought decides a valium will do the trick. It puts me straight to sleep until I wake up to the noise of a rocket shooting through the room. I leap out of bed, shaking uncontrollably, running from room to room. The rocket had passed over the building, but I had thought it was right beside me. Blood is dripping from my hand, but I don't know how I cut myself. I manage to dress in spite of my confused state of mind and go down to the neighbours' below, where, without so much as a 'by your leave', I take another valium and go to sleep.

I wake up at 7.30 in the morning to the sound of the inferno outside. I had slept straight through the naval and artillery bombardment, and even through the air raids which began at six in the morning. I give myself a shake and pull myself together. This is no time for hysterics, and certainly no time to start a nervous breakdown. There will be enough time for that later, if I stay alive.

CHAPTER 15

It's Thursday August 12th. The Israelis have got us used to air raids on Wednesdays and Sundays and sometimes on Tuesdays and Fridays, but this is our first Thursday. It must be a special occasion! I slept through sixty air raids this morning. Now I join in the desperate running from room to room, and floor to floor, but I refuse to go down to the shelter. The screams of those trapped in the shelter of the vacuum-bombed building are still vivid in my mind.

To think that all this is taking place because a few katyousha rockets landed in the Galilee. I know that may be bad from the Israelis' point of view, but does it excuse the cluster bombs, the phosphorus shells, the vacuum bomb, the air raids, the

115

thousands of dead and maimed? If it does then I don't think much of world opinion. I am angry and frustrated; I have never killed anyone and I don't see why I and hundreds of thousands of innocent people should be butchered for Menahem Begin.

Let's take this so-called 'Operation Peace for Galilee' right from the beginning. It started with two incidents: the assassination attempt on the Israeli Ambassador to London and some katyoushas in the Galilee. (But the only attacks on Galilee since the Israeli-Palestinian ceasefire arranged by Philip Habib in July 1981 were two last May and June in retaliation for Israeli air raids. And the attack on the Ambassador was carried out by a group that had broken away from the PLO.) The 'Operation' was supposed to take the Israelis 45 kilometres into Lebanon to clear that part of the country of the Palestinian 'terrorists'. Today the Israeli Defence Forces have reached Byblos and are pushing further into North Lebanon; the Tsahal is 132 kilometres from the Lebanese-Israeli border, and 85 kilometres from its original goal. On June 4th, Israel Radio had named the invasion 'Operation Cedar', and only some hours later did it become 'Operation Peace for Galilee'. Was that just to camouflage an advance right to the cedars of Lebanon, the symbol of its independence and civilisation? I'll wait and see.

As I write I remember a joke that went around a couple of years ago, when the Syrians and Phalangists fell out so badly. It was not a new joke, but was adapted to the situation. Three men travelling in a car from Tripoli to Beirut were stopped at a Syrian barricade. 'Don't worry,' the Syrian said, 'All I want is to look at your identity cards.' The cards were promptly brought out.

'Now,' said the Syrian, 'I'll ask each of you a question. If you can answer it, you go free; if not, you're under arrest. Don't worry, the question will be easy. You, first. Let's see, your name is Muhammad Ahmad Mustapha. Here's the question: early this century a huge ship called the Titanic had twelve hundred passengers on board; it ran into an iceberg and sank. What was the name of the ship?'

'The Titanic,' sighed Muhammad Ahmad Mustapha in relief.

'Good. You can go. Now let's see the next one. Your name is Mahmoud Muhammad. Why are you shaking like that? Don't worry, your question is easy. The Titanic had twelve hundred passengers on board. How many passengers was she carrying?'

'Twelve hundred!'

'Great, you've passed the test. Let's see your friend now. Your identity card? I see, your name is Maroun Maroun. Don't worry, your question is just as simple, Maroun. There was a ship called the Titanic, she carried twelve hundred passengers. All you have to do is give me their names and addresses!'

I remember this story today because of what is happening to us, this Thursday August 12th, as the Kfirs and Mirages fly over. Just yesterday we thought negotiations had been successfully concluded, but Israel's conditions have changed so often since the beginning of the invasion. Let's review them in chronological order: the Palestinians' katyoushas must be out of reach of the Galilee; Christian Phalangists must be installed in their place wherever possible, if not then Saad Haddad's men; the Palestinian armed elements must leave Beirut; Palestinian armed elements must leave Lebanon unconditionally; the Palestinians can leave with their individual weapons; Israel must have the number of those leaving; the Palestinians' departure must be simultaneous with the entry of the multinational forces; no, the multinationals can only come in after half the Palestinians have left; Israel wants the return of the corpses of eight soldiers killed in 1978; the Syrians must leave along with the Palestinians; Israel wants eight thousand Palestinians to leave, not seven thousand two hundred as had been suggested. Now Israel wants the names of all those leaving and their destination.

So tomorrow Israel may ask for the addresses of the eight thousand and the day after the names of their children.

To add insult to injury, Philip Habib wants an immediate answer to the Israeli demands from Prime Minister Chafic Wazzan, although he can see and hear the non-stop air raids over West Beirut. Premier Wazzan angrily refuses to continue the negotiations, and is backed by former premiers Saeb Salam and Selim al-Hoss, as well as by the National Movement. 'How can I negotiate when my own people are being butchered right before my eyes?' Wazzan asks.

Before this murderous Thursday, two countries had offered to take in all the Palestinians: Syria and Tunisia. Tunisian President Habib Bourguiba even sent a cable to Yasser Arafat

117

saying, 'Even though you were against us a few years ago [Bourguiba had always maintained the Arabs should accept the UN partition plan of 1947], we open our hearts and homes to you and all your people.' We understood the negotiations were over, and D-Day was to have been Saturday, the day of the Palestinians' departure. But Israel wanted the Palestinians to leave before the multinational forces came in, and was asking for D-Day plus three days; it later asked for D-Day plus seven. Premier Wazzan insisted the two D-Days should coincide, and all this while we were being hit.

I think it is obvious that Sharon wants the Palestinians either not to come out alive, or to come out crawling. That is difficult to accept. Even the battered West Beirutis who wanted just one thing a month ago—the Palestinians' departure, so they would no longer be hit—will not accept this. Saeb Salam and the National Movement vehemently expressed the opinion of West Beirut, that the Palestinians must leave with dignity and honour.

A few days ago, Amin Gemayel—Bashir Gemayel's brother—came to visit West Beirut and left taking Georgina Rizk and her little son with him. Georgina, the former Miss Universe who focused world attention on Lebanon when she was elected, had married Abou Hassan Salameh, one of Arafat's closest advisors. Salameh had long since been assassinated by Mossad agents. Georgina had tried to leave West Beirut during the siege, but the Phalangists told her she would have to leave her two-year-old Palestinian son behind, so she stayed. When Amin Gemayel came and took them out he warned all those he met in West Beirut that Thursday August 12th would be bad. No one believed him until today; but no one could have done anything anyway.

I feel exhausted, partly because of the breakdown I had yesterday, but the air raids have forced me to try to appear cool and collected. No one is ever going to say Lina Mikdadi was scared. I am very scared, but there's no need to show it, is there?

I hear that D-Day has been postponed from Saturday to Monday. I also hear that they've caught the man who identified for the Israelis the building they vacuum-bombed. Little good that does the two hundred and fifty innocent people who died. But so many buildings have come crashing down since that day that I have lost count. I've seen the devastation with my own eyes. The hospital where Dr Amal Shamma (the American citizen who sent Reagan that letter on July 4th) worked day and night has had to close its doors. A few floors of the Bristol Hotel have been turned into a hospital.

We've had our fill of rice—I swear I'll never eat rice again when the war is over, that is if I'm still alive. The kilo of potatoes that used to sell for two Lebanese pounds a month ago now costs 25 pounds (approximately $6) if you can find any. A kilo of tomatoes also costs 25 pounds, and a kilo of lemons has gone up from two to 60 pounds. A gallon of fuel has shot up from 32 to 250 pounds when available. And people still buy. Where the heck do they get the cash? I have almost run out of money with barely 150 pounds left, and there are no banks open.

But we manage, and sometimes we even get that rarity of rarities, fruit, through friends who smuggle it from East Beirut in their official cars. We're not starving yet, but I am sure some people are, so every morning I go around with a few packages and whenever anyone asks I give them away.

Today I found a family standing in the street with their luggage waiting for a car to pick them up. I had never seen them before, but I stopped and asked:

'Why are you leaving?'

'We're scared.'

'Please stay.'

'We can't, we're sorry. We can't take it any more.'

'Please, please stay, everything is going to be all right!'

'We can't, we're sorry,' the woman said tearfully. I stood on the pavement and cried openly while they hurriedly stuffed their things into the car and went on their way, wishing me good luck.

At three o'clock on this bloody Thursday, the President of the Chamber of Deputies, Mr Kamel al-Assaad, is playing tennis with friends at the summer resort of Broummana in the East. Here the sky is filled with Kfirs and Mirages, and buildings collapse like packs of cards.

Suddenly, at five o'clock there is not a sound in West Beirut; after two hundred and twenty air raids, after five hundred people have been killed or maimed for life, the eleventh cease-fire has gone into effect. We don't yet know whether to believe

119

it; maybe it's just a break for the Israeli pilots who have been bombing us for eleven hours nonstop. Ariel Sharon says today's air raids were meant to speed up the political negotiations; he has asked no one's permission to go into action; he has not even consulted the Israeli cabinet.

At 5.05, Radio Lebanon announces that President Kamel al-Assaad has set a date for the presidential elections: Thursday August 19th. We make no comment, we are simply too exhausted. But then, he hasn't asked our opinion; he doesn't seem to consider West Beirut to be part of Lebanon. Al-Assaad asks Premier Wazzan to get the Israeli forces out of the area around the parliament so elections can be held. Wazzan answers privately, 'I don't know if I'll be able to reach my own home tomorrow, let alone liberate the Chamber of Deputies!'

The only candidate is still Bashir Gemayel, who has not raised his voice against the Israeli invasion, because it suited him, or against the siege of Beirut. Of the 92 deputies remaining in parliament, 47 are out of the country. One of these is Joseph Skaff, our Defence Minister, who, I am told, has kidney trouble. We are a country at war without a defence minister. I find that very funny, but then Lebanon is a funny country.

It looks as if the next six years will be spent under Phalangist rule. Bashir Gemayel has a good chance of becoming President and seems to enjoy the support of certain foreign powers. But this is a man who fought in one part of Lebanon against the other part; how can it work? If anyone asked them, the people of Lebanon would say they wanted someone strong and firm and just, someone who hasn't been physically involved in the seven-year civil war; but no one has asked the people. After all, we have a parliament which is supposed to represent us and elect a president. The parliament, made up of ninety-nine members, is supposed to be elected every four years; the last elections were in 1972, when the vast majority of the previous parliament was returned.

Many things happened in the '70s. The beginning of the decade saw the Black September clashes in Jordan which caused the PLO to come to Lebanon; Egypt's President Abdel-Nasser died; and we had a new president, Suleiman Franjiye. In succeeding years, the war in Vietnam ended, the October 1973 war was fought between Arabs and Israelis, Saudi Arabia's King Feysal was assassinated, the Lebanese civil war broke out,

Anwar Sadat visited Jerusalem, the Israelis invaded Lebanon, the siege of Beirut began. In the meantime, not one member of our parliament has changed. Six have died of sickness or old age and one admirable man has been assassinated—Kamal Joumblatt, father of Walid Joumblatt, who formed the Lebanese National Movement.

Seven down, ninety-two to go, for Lebanon to be rid of its ten-year-old parliament. But no one seems inclined to move of their own accord and parliamentary elections are unlikely to be held in the near future. The same people who elected Presidents Franjiye and Sarkis are about to elect yet another president. This is some democracy! Some vote out of principle, some for the money it brings them, and some under pressure, it's the same story every six years. With such a parliament and the prospect of Shaikh Bashir as President, I don't see how peace can come to Lebanon.

I love peace as much as the next person, but not peace under pressure. You can't force peace on people; you can bring it about slowly and gently, by giving people time to forget and forgive. What kind of peace is possible in Lebanon today, where Christian Phalangists and Druze are at each other's throats in the mountains, and where the Lebanese Forces (namely the Phalangists) can take over Lebanese army barracks without a second thought? In the East they go to the beach, jog, play tennis, eat in restaurants, laugh and joke, while in the West their own people, Muslim and Christian, are being butchered by a supposedly common enemy. How will it be possible to go back to the old times and unite again? Aren't the Lebanese in the East part of us? Don't they feel anything towards us but indifference?

Thursday August 12th, 1982: a day that will be recorded as one of the bloodiest in the siege. After 220 Israeli air raids; after eleven hours of non-stop combat; after 44,000 bombs had been dropped on West Beirut, destroying 800 homes and causing 500 casualties, a phone call was made at 4.45 in the afternoon. Reagan said to Begin: this had better stop. It will, said Begin. It had better! Reagan said. This was why you could have heard a pin drop at five o'clock in West Beirut. President Reagan, may I ask you a question: why didn't you make your phone call earlier?

CHAPTER 16

Today, it seems that congratulations are in order: the Palestinians are leaving Lebanon, the Israelis are staying. As for the Syrians, they have already withdrawn from some regions. And the Lebanese? Some are fools who don't see the danger in what is happening, others do and walk around like zombies. As for me, I feel sad and bewildered. I haven't recovered from yesterday's air raids, or Wednesday's tension, and I am not too happy about today's date: Friday the 13th! But I have washed my hair, which is an accomplishment. I even managed to change my jeans, and that's another.

Friday and Saturday are two days of almost complete quiet. The effect in West Beirut is eerie. The banging of a door makes us all jump. I try to look and sound normal, but without much success: my nerves are on edge, and I feel dizzy. I can't go to sleep so I go out on my usual rounds.

The destruction is widespread. One man who has just come back from checking his home can barely walk.

'What's wrong?'

'My home.'

'What about it?'

'The whole building is on the ground.'

'But you're still alive, you'll build another one.'

He doesn't reply and walks away like someone in a dream. A home is the symbol of security, and he's lost that. Hundreds of thousands of people have. I notice that people are more controlled when the fierce battles are on; it's only when there's quiet that reality hits them, and hits them hard. Then the suppressed anxiety, fear and despair surface. Children still laugh, but the sound of their laughter is hollow. Jokes are still made, but they're macabre and sickening. One woman I know who has always been well-mannered and well-bred tells me today: 'You can burp, fart, curse and swear. Everything is allowed now that there's a war.'

For this woman to use such words shows that she's half-crazed with fear. I try to calm her down by describing a scene I saw this morning: a woman was bathing her two little children at one of the broken pipes on the pavement, scrubbing them for all she was worth. The sight moved me very much: it was both pathetic and full of hope. But the woman doesn't react.

I try to explain that she's much better off than the 250 old people still in the Islamic home which has been half-destroyed by bombs. From the staff of 200 only 18 had stayed to take care of them and, walking through the damaged building, you can barely see the patients through the clouds of flies covering them. But the woman's eyes have a faraway look; she's not listening.

'Don't,' she says.

'You don't want to hear about the misery around you?'

'Don't bang your foot against the table!'

Her nerves are shattered so I try to cheer her up by telling her about today's big explosion in the mountains which killed and wounded three Israelis. I repeat the rumour that the Baader Meinhoff people have kidnapped five Israeli officers in East Beirut.

'What, what did you just say?' she shouts. I tell the stories again.

'My God, my God, they're going to bomb us again,' she wails, 'Oh, my God.' She starts to recite prayers from the Quran and continues to wail for a long time. This woman will really need a long, long rest when the war is over.

In another incident today, one Israeli soldier was killed and another captured when they lost their way in the mountains and entered Syrian territory. Meanwhile, Ambassador Paul Marc Henry of France is a little bewildered. He has just learned that Menahem Begin refuses to call the day of the Palestinians' departure D-Day, which is too reminiscent of Allied victories in World War II. He wants it changed to E-Day, 'E' for evacuation, which would spell defeat.

'Don't find us, we'll find you.' That's the motto of the Palestinians these days. Even their allies can't find them. They have gone underground and are nowhere to be seen. They send messages to their friends, cables to Arab leaders and letters to the press, but no one knows from where. One young man, Seif, made it his hobby to look for them; he was a great friend of Yasser Arafat's and felt left out. The other day he tracked down the PLO leader at his newest hiding place and arrived there the same time Arafat did. Seif looked triumphant, and Arafat surprised. Seif then lost Arafat for twenty-four hours, and Abou Ammar said jokingly, 'If Seif can't find me, then nobody can!' I am told Seif is still looking.

There is an American fact-finding mission in West Beirut; they want to talk. 'Talk about what?' I ask them. 'If you want to find facts go and tour West Beirut and see for yourselves. The economic infrastructure of the country has been destroyed. Not a school has been spared, not a factory, hospital, hotel, ministry or home. Just get into a car and drive around. Then you can go back to the United States and say that you saw for yourselves, not that you were told by people under stress who lacked objectivity. Go, and good luck to you!'

Mother Theresa is here, the Nobel Peace Prize winner. She is staying in a convent in the East, but she did visit us for a few hours. She took back with her thirty children who had been in the destroyed mental home and who were being looked after by Fateh (the main PLO guerrilla group). The children have become uncontrollable because of the shelling; no one knows what medicine to give them because they've chewed away their wrist-bands. No one knows their names, or anything about them. They were being kept in the refugee camps and there are still fifty left in Sabra, Chatila and Bourj Brajneh, the areas hardest hit by the Israelis. These have been Palestinian refugee areas almost since Israel was created. Now Bashir Gemayel's Radio Free Lebanon refers to them as 'military camps' although Israel Radio still calls them refugee camps!

There is now a cat at the Ministry of Tourism. She came in on the day of the vacuum bomb. She can't stand any kind of noise, small or loud. We named her Hissar (siege) and kept her. I have made new friends other than Hissar. The building where I live has become one big family, including the doorman and his wife Amina. She is pregnant—she thinks it's been nine months, but she probably has no idea of how long it really is— and she is barely fifteen years old and very scared. 'Don't worry, I'll help with the birth,' I tell her reassuringly every morning, but she doesn't seem reassured. Amina will have to give birth in the doorman's little room. Her husband will not allow her to be touched by any other man; they're from Kurdistan and extremely conservative. All the women in the building are willing to assist in the delivery.

As I write I hear the planes pass over us. Sometimes I try to make believe that they're commercial flights. They seem to

124

be getting lower and I don't like that at all, although I'm told they're just reconaissance flights. We West Beirutis have become experts in military science. We can tell a Kfir from a Mirage, a Skyhawk from an F-15 just by the sound they make. Thank you, General Sharon, for these lessons.

The buzzing in the sky has made me lose my wits again. This makes me angry: it has taken me the last forty-eight hours to pick up the pieces of my shattered brain and achieve a semblance of normality. I think I can hear a helicopter—or is it only the sound of a generator? My God, I think I'm losing my mind, like I did last Sunday night when I went out on the balcony and saw hundreds of flare bombs. I started screaming in panic: 'A parachute, a parachute!' They tried to calm me down: 'It's all right, each flare bomb is dropped by parachute.' It looked like the parachute was heading straight towards me, and it took time to calm my fit of hysterics.

Today, Sunday 15th, is a day of rest from the shelling, but not from looters. They're systematically emptying every apartment they can get into. I watch in rage and frustration as some of them throw my friends' things out of the windows of their flat nearby. There's nothing I can do.

'What the hell are they going to do with all this stuff?' I ask. 'They can't get out of West Beirut.'

'Oh, they'll store it until the siege is over,' someone replies, 'then sell it somewhere else.' My aunt's house has been broken into and looted, and I can't get to it—it's only a hundred metres from the Israeli positions.

Monday August 16th is the beginning of a crucial week for both the Lebanese and the Palestinians. Optimism and pessimism come and go in waves: departure day is near and so is election day. Israel has not attacked for the past three days, but the calm is still disquieting; the planes continue to pass over on their reconaissance flights. Israel has accepted the Lebanese conditions transmitted by Philip Habib. Begin no longer wants the names of those leaving; the Palestinians don't have to go by sea, they can take the Beirut-Damascus road; the Palestinians can withdraw simultaneously with the arrival of the multinational forces. I wonder to whom we owe all this generosity?

The Lebanese are concerned about the elections—there's still only one serious candidate, Bashir Gemayel. How can a president be elected with most of the country occupied by Israel? How democratic is the procedure if there's only one candidate? It has been decided that sixty-two deputies will be enough for a quorum, and that forty-seven votes are needed to elect a president. There are forty-eight hours to go before the elections, so let's wait and see.

The West Beirutis continue to survive. Like all the Lebanese we have a vitality no one can crush. We look both ways to cross a one-way street; we've become very good at hauling gallons of water and fuel; we're excellent treasure hunters. Although there is very little here, we still manage to find things: vegetables, fruit, meat, poultry.

I hear that the Palestinians are leaving towards the end of this week, and that the Americans, the French and the Italians are coming. So next week it will be Hi, Bonjour and Ciao! We've had quite a few languages to learn in the last decade, but we're bright and adaptable.

Now D-Day is thirty-six hours away, A-Day ('A' for arrival) is seventy-two hours away, and E-Day ('E' for elections) is barely eighteen hours away. I don't know what's going to happen tomorrow, but the plot is thickening. I'm told the Israelis originally wanted to invade Lebanon in February but delayed their plans to help the elections along. Well, someone seems to know what's going to happen: this morning the Phalangists' Radio Free Lebanon said Shaikh Bashir had issued orders to the Lebanese Forces and the inhabitants of 'Free Lebanon', forbidding anyone to shoot in celebration, whatever the reason. He seems sure of the outcome.

We've been through a lot in the past seventy-six days and suffered a great deal, but I don't think we've seen anything yet compared to what's coming. Why are the elections taking place before the Palestinians withdraw? Why are the multinational forces arriving afterwards? How can elections be held under Israeli occupation and what do the Israelis plan to do then? D-Day, A-Day and E-Day seem to be preparing the ground for something else.

Meanwhile, the Israelis are installing central heating in the mountains. Some people in the mountain town of Aley asked the Israelis what their intentions were. An Israeli colonel answered haughtily, 'I'm not here to discuss things with you; I'm here to tell you what to do.' A woman in West Beirut called up a friend in the East, a Mr Salam, to invite him to lunch. A man on the other end of the line said roughly, 'This is East Beirut, we don't have any Muslims here!' A good omen for unity between East and West.

A friend of mine who had very long, lovely hair had it cut really short this morning.

'What did you do that for?' I asked her.

'So that I won't pull my hair out on Thursday!' she replied seriously.

I miss Leyla and Rasha. I haven't seen them for twenty-nine days: I count the days although no one thinks I do. I close my eyes and try to see their faces in my mind, but I can't. I still go to their house every day, but never into their rooms. It's six o'clock in the afternoon: the sky is light blue and pink, powdered with a few white clouds. We've still had no visitors from outer space, just a couple of supersonic booms. Today there are more fruits and vegetables, and even a little water, but we still have no electricity to pump it up.

Some horses have appeared in the public gardens. They graze on the remaining grass, a strangely peaceful tableau. I wish I had the courage to shoot one of them. He's a lovely beast but he has a broken leg and the children who live in the gardens treat him like a new toy. I yell at them to leave him alone, but in vain.

Seven years of war have brought us to this: we do a lot of talking, but never act; we sit and hope for the best and get nothing but the worst; we rely on people and get slapped in the face. I don't want to hear anything ever again about the Steadfastness and Confrontation Front (formed by six Arab countries and the PLO to oppose peace with Israel following Sadat's visit to Jerusalem). These countries' armies could have wiped out part of Israel while its Defence Forces were busy with Lebanon, but they preferred to sit back and give us advice on how to sacrifice our blood for the Palestinian cause.

I have some advice for you: don't tell us what to do, get ready yourselves because next time it may be your turn. You saw it on television when there was nothing else to watch. What did the people in your countries think, gentlemen, when they saw the effect of a vacuum bomb—or are they not allowed to think? Did it ever occur to you that this might happen to your country one day? Or do you believe you have nothing to do with the Arab cause? Or that you are above reproach? God help those who ever turn to you for help.

There are twelve more hours to E-Day. So far fifty-eight members of parliament plan to attend the session, and thirty-four have decided to boycott it. Muslim leaders met in Saeb Salam's house this morning and decided they wanted a President who had not been involved in the civil war. They said normal elections could not be held under occupation, and called for unity between Muslims and Christians. Tomorrow we will see if this meeting has had any impact. A quorum will not be reached if only fifty-eight deputies attend, but the night is long and so much can happen.

I have no idea what the future holds for Lebanon. I am tired and nervous, drink and nibble at anything; I'm not especially kind to people. The Lebanese have had to buy new sofas for the parliament's reception room because the old ones were taken by the Israelis. They cost 13,000 Lebanese pounds.

It's now around eleven o'clock at night. All is quiet except for the noise of the generators. I'm writing by gaslight—I've learned how to use it since my first disastrous experience. At 11.15 Parliament Speaker Kamel al-Assaad announces that the elections have been postponed for 'security reasons' (some people think it is because a quorum had not been reached). The meeting will now be held on Monday at the same time, but it has been moved to a 'safer' place—the army barracks in Feyadieh to the east of Beirut. So much for the reception room sofas! According to Article 26 of the Constitution, presidential elections must take place in the capital, but that's no problem— Feyadieh has suddenly become part of Beirut!

On Thursday August 19th I go on my rounds while people hold secret meetings to prepare for the elections: I'm sure envelopes sometimes change hands. Rumour has it that the Saudi Ambassador is coming back to Beirut after months of absence. I wonder whether the Saudis want Shaikh Bashir or not. Everybody elects the president in Lebanon—the Americans, the Saudis, the Syrians, the Israelis, even the members of the Lebanese parliament—everybody except the people of Lebanon.

At 1.45 in the afternoon, a pretty young brunette stops at the entrance to the underground garage of the Ministries of Information and Tourism. The soldiers ask her for identification and she hands it to them. They open the gate for her—she is an employee of the Ministry of Information. She parks the car and calmly walks back up. 'Where are you going?' one of the guards asks her. 'To see Minister Hamade's secretary Renée,' she replies. Two minutes later, the same guard notices the girl walking briskly away; she hasn't had time to see anyone. He rushes up to see Renée, who shouts excitedly that she is not expecting anyone, that she doesn't know anyone who has a green Volvo.

The girl is caught sauntering down Hamra Street in search of a telephone, and brought back to her car where men have already started dismantling the door panels. They find 120 kilogrammes of TNT, 60 of Hexogen and 32 detonators: enough to blow up several buildings as well as the Ministry and all the people in it, including the ministers of information, social affairs and tourism, and a few important members of the Lebanese National Movement.

The girl's papers are forged, but we still don't know who sent her. Who could have planned such a thing? Who has the most interest in getting rid of these people? What kind of democracy is this?

Let me pass on a couple of pieces of advice I've learned from this siege. During bombing, stay where you are; don't run down to the shelters; wait to see what happens and swallow a stiff drink. During elections, don't meddle, don't give your opinion, whether for or against; discussing politics may be hazardous to your health; talk instead of the bombing, the weather, the latest fashions. Democracy in Lebanon has reached the pits. I have a friend who is half-Lebanese, half-Haitian. She had two brothers who were assassinated by Papa Doc's Tonton Macoutes, but now she claims she wants to go back to Haiti.

'*Kennst du das Land, wo die. . .*' 'Know you the land where the lemon trees bloom? In the dark foliage the golden oranges glow; a soft wind blows from the heavens, the myrtle is still and the laurel stands tall—do you know it well? There, there I would go.' That is how I would like Lebanon to be. That is how I hope it will be in the future.

The future is the future and today is today. The two daily newspapers whose offices were hit by rockets—*Al-Nahar* and its sister French paper *L'Orient-Le Jour*—have reappeared today, along with eggs, more vegetables and fruit. That's not bad. On the other hand, another time bomb has been found, near a bank in West Beirut. It was defused, but some day one will explode, and that helps to keep the West Beirutis' nerves on edge.

Operation D-Day is about to begin. The Palestinians are to leave on Saturday August 21st to Athens and Larnaca by boat. The Italians are to come in on the same day; Reagan has agreed to a request to send 800 marines, and the French are also sending 800 troops. The captured Israeli pilot (and another soldier who was captured while he sauntered drunkenly into a southern Lebanese village) are to be handed over to Israel with the corpses of the nine soldiers killed in 1978. The Lebanese say they have already been handed over to the International Red Cross, the Israelis say they haven't; the Red Cross say nothing.

I let these events take care of themselves while I go through West Beirut on my daily tasks. I've been asked by the Arab-American Anti-Discrimination Committee to find fifty children who have been severely wounded or have lost a limb in the shelling; the Committee will take them to Washington for treatment at its expense. I work on this for most of the day; there are still good people in the world and just knowing that makes me feel much better.

In the evening I call my father and step-mother in Switzerland to see if they're still all right. They seem so far away, like Leyla and Rasha. Dear God, I miss their laughter, their jokes, their quarrels and their mess; dear God, allow me to live to see my children again. It is amazing that you can still get an international line (I have direct dialling thanks to Marwan) when it is difficult to call anyone inside West Beirut, or in the East and other parts of Lebanon; it is surprising that with all the bombing any lines still work. When I speak to my father, I pretend I am fine; I feel scared, but I can't bring myself to tell him; I feel depressed, but I say nothing; I am filled with anguish and despair, but I don't want to worry him.

There is a new moon tonight: it looks pure and beautiful. May it symbolise a new start for Lebanon. I can hear the muezzins' call to prayer from minarets all over West Beirut. It sounds like the old days when they called to prayer without loudspeakers. I can hear a church bell peal in the distance.

Everything seems so normal. Please God, we've had enough; let things be normal again. I know I sound childish and stupid, but I feel so desperate—and yet, I don't want to leave.

By eleven o'clock at night, Beirut is noisy again. Shooting has broken out near the seafront and there are a few explosions in the distance. I don't know what is happening, and I'm too tired to find out. I review the day's events in my mind: some deputies have gone underground. They don't want to vote for Shaikh Bashir and don't want to come under pressure; they want a president who can heal the wounds, not one who has taken part in causing them, a compromise candidate. Tension has been rising all day, with the first batch of Palestinians due to leave tomorrow. The telephone lines between East and West Beirut have been cut so deputies and officials cannot discuss the elections. The Saudi Ambassador hasn't come back after all; he will come after the elections.

The Israelis now say they have received the two Israeli soldiers held by the Palestinians as well as the nine corpses. The captured Israeli pilot had earlier made three requests of the Palestinians: to see Yasser Arafat, to donate blood to both Palestinians and Lebanese wounded in the air raids, and, if released, not to be sent to Syria. 'That makes two of us,' a Palestinian leader told him jokingly.

Raymond Eddé, the Lebanese leader in exile in Paris, has said he wants to come back. He should have come back a long time ago; he would have made a good president. Honesty and integrity are his main qualities, and both are badly needed.

Philip Habib sounds like he has had enough. He tells anyone who'll listen that he has nothing to do with the presidential elections. I wonder if there is anything he can possibly do about the eight thousand Lebanese and Palestinian prisoners held by the Israelis in the prison camp they have built at the town of Ansar in South Lebanon. Meanwhile, the United Nations has renewed the mandate of the UN troops in the South (UNIFIL) for another two months.

Prime Minister Chafic Wazzan delivered a speech today to the top officers in the Lebanese army, the ones who are supposed to be coming into West Beirut when the Palestinians leave. He reminded them of their oath and of their major aim: to protect Lebanon and the Lebanese. You can sense a certain reproach, reading between the lines. The army has done nothing so far to defend West Beirut and its inhabitants.

'Young men. . . Go on your mission with God's blessing. . . The nation looks to you and your success,' Wazzan said. 'On the morrow, when you see destruction in the buildings and the streets, remember that you have arms to help; if you see suffering on the faces of the people, remember that you carry a part of Lebanon's heart within you that may cleanse that pain with love; if you see a fierce person before you, deal with him swiftly. The time has come for the cruel to disappear forever. . .

'Go with God's blessing, and if you see the burnt pine trees of Beirut remember that those trees were offered in sacrifice to the nation's honour, to save the cedar tree, our country's symbol. Long live Lebanon.'

CHAPTER 17

The Palestinians have started to leave: it is Saturday August 21st. I wake up in the morning to the sound of farewell shooting as the 420-strong Badr battalion tours the streets of West Beirut to bid a last goodbye to the people who helped them. The West Beirutis stand on their balconies, throwing rice at the departing soldiers and crying.

Are you happy now, those of you who wanted them to go? Was there anything the Palestinians could have done in the face of the international plot to annihilate them which began in September 1970 in Jordan? And was their part in the civil war of Lebanon in 1975 really as significant as all that? Today, as they board the boat that will take them to Larnaca on their way to Jordan, the Lebanese are more divided than ever. There were civil wars in Lebanon before 1975, when there were no Palestinians around. Lebanon will shortly discover that its problem is between the Lebanese.

Walid Joumblatt is at home when the Badr battalion passes his house to bid him farewell. Joumblatt is asked to protect the wives and children they leave behind. He cannot stop his tears from flowing although he tries to put on a brave front.

In my heart I bid farewell to you, the heroes of a nation that has not seen the light of day since 1948, to you who helped Beirut during its siege by the Israelis and others. But I'll never say goodbye to the revolution you created; it will survive. The Israeli victory is hollow; the Palestinian cause still lives wherever the Palestinians are. May those who died rest in peace, those who survived will take over their mission. Go, with God's blessing, believe in Him and in your just cause. You go with pain in your hearts, but also with joy; 'Operation Annihilation' has not succeeded.

I hear there's going to be an Arab summit in Morocco. What for? Haven't we seen enough of the Arabs in action in the past seventy-seven days?

Today is Sunday August 22nd. Yesterday I cried and cried, like I did when my mother died; I couldn't stop the heart-breaking sobs. I cried for the injustice in the world, for the Lebanese and Palestinians alike, for the 'V' for Victory sign the Palestinians made as they left, which was nothing but a show of defiance. Of the 400 due to leave yesterday, two didn't show up and one was wounded by a stray bullet; the remaining 397 are now in Jordan and Iraq.

This morning another thousand are leaving, to Tunisia. I pick up the pieces of my broken heart and go to Corniche Mazraa to bid them farewell; many citizens of West Beirut have done the same. Women lean out of windows that no longer have any panes to throw rice; they wave from half-destroyed balconies. Many cry as they watch the trucks go by. The Palestinians have already said goodbye to their children, wives and parents at the municipal stadium. Some tried to joke when they said goodbye to their families: 'I have my bathing-suit on under my uniform. I can't wait to reach the boat to get a suntan.'

I wonder what names the boats have that are taking them away: they all spell 'exodus' to me. Two little boys in full battle-dress, carrying a kalashnikov each, are leaving with their father today. Their mother was killed in the shelling, and they have no one to stay with. I feel numb all over, and barely notice the spent bullets falling down around me. The people watching the poignant scenes look as devastated as the buildings around them.

Another batch leaves tomorrow, for the two Yemens. Every day a batch is shipped like sacks of flour. Many Lebanese are overjoyed at the Palestinians' departure, and have opened bottles of champagne, some in secret, others openly. I prefer the latter, it is more honest. I heard a neighbour of mine turn to some of his friends and comment loudly: 'Good riddance to bad rubbish. May God thank you, Bashir Gemayel, we're well rid of these bastards.' To each his opinion, I thought; that is real democracy.

The Greek boat with a thousand Palestinians on board finally left at 8.45 this evening because of an argument between the Palestinians and Israelis over some jeeps taken on board. The issue was finally resolved by Philip Habib, and the vessel left still carrying the jeeps.

It is a fourth exodus for the Palestinians: from Palestine in 1948; from Jerusalem, the West Bank and the Gaza strip in 1967; from Jordan in 1970; and from Lebanon in August 1982 on to North and South Yemen, Iraq, Jordan, Syria and Tunisia. Next year in Jerusalem.

In all the commotion of the Palestinians' departure, some of us have forgotten an important event: the Lebanese presidential elections tomorrow, Monday. Former premier Saeb Salam is one of those against holding them now. He wants to find a compromise candidate. In an interview on Lebanese television, Salam said, 'I am for having a Maronite president to give the Christians a guarantee. It is a regrettable fact that obstacles have been built between the Lebanese, that roads have been closed, and phone links cut. Members of Parliament have been forbidden to pass from one region to another; this is unacceptable. Everyone knows that my candidate would be Raymond Eddé but, despite my feelings about him, I will forgo this candidature; I will even accept an extension of President Sarkis's mandate. There must be a Muslim-Christian understanding; there must not be a victor and vanquished. Lebanon must remain a country based on understanding and love.'

Bashir Gemayel, on the other hand, is certain the session will take place on Monday: 'I have contacted many deputies and they have assured me they will attend although some of them may not vote for me. I thank them all—may the best candidate win.'

Raymond Eddé says in an interview that some deputies have contacted him and told him they had been threatened to attend or else. Meanwhile, according to a poll conducted by the Israelis in a town in the Chouf, the most popular president would be Raymond Eddé!

As for the deputies, Mounir Abou Fadel, for example, does

not want to attend. Six years ago Abou Fadel had refused to go to parliament to vote under pressure from Saiqa (the Syrian-backed Palestinian group which brought Sarkis to power). He says he is not against anyone in particular, but wants understanding and co-operation between the parties concerned before there is an election. He is still refusing to go, even though he found several shotguns in his car a few days ago and has received threatening phone calls.

A Sunni deputy, Hassan Rifai, was shot and wounded in his home town in the Bekaa this morning. He said from his hospital bed in Damascus that he was shot because he didn't want to attend the session.

Shaikh Pierre Gemayel, founder of the Phalangists, wants a strong regime based on unity and coexistence. Deputy Najah Wakim accuses some of his colleagues of having received millions of dollars just to attend the session.

In the mountain town of Aley, nine Druze were assassinated today; later seven Christians were killed in Kfarmatta, a few kilometres away. Most of the Palestinians are gone and the Lebanese are still fighting; now terrorism seems to be the name of the game.

There is nothing but chaos in the country. Sarkis Naoum, a commentator in *Al-Nahar,* blames it on Arab indifference. I couldn't agree with him more. Where are you, the Arabs from the Gulf to those in North Africa? Are you too busy counting your pennies or sunbathing on the beach with your beloved while here we have been separated from ours for God knows how long?

Where are you, President Reagan? I hear you have the picture of four-month-old Elias whose arms were amputated after a round of Israeli bombing. An important part of the oath of allegiance to the American flag goes 'and justice for all'. Does this only apply to the Israelis and people like them? Aren't we human beings too?

At last, it is Monday August 23rd. I have all the papers in front of me by eight o'clock in the morning and I am trying to get a sense of what will happen when parliament meets at eleven. Here are some of the headlines:

'Presidential elections today: one or two members in the balance for quorum'—*Al-Nahar* (independent).

'The day of constitutional rights is here. Al-Assaad: the

boycott has been dropped'—*Al-Amal* (Phalangist).

'Parliament to elect new president: Bashir Gemayel assured; quorum reached'—*Le Reveil* (Phalangist).

'Muslim and Nationalist boycott will explode the session—Phalangists increase efforts to win presidency by force'—*As-Safir* (nationalist).

'The candidate of occupation—from terrorism to assassination. Hassan Rifai: the Phalangists tried to assassinate me to lower number of quorum'—*An-Nida* (Communist).

'Muftis Khaled (Sunni) and Shamseddine (Shia) call for postponement of sessions for fear of partition'—*Al-Liwa* (pro-Iraq).

It is 10.30, and I wait. Yesterday we had electricity for a few hours, no vegetables, and a lot of explosions. Today we have no electricity, no vegetables, little water and no phones. The presidential elections are to take place in thirty minutes while the siege of West Beirut continues.

By 1.50 in the afternoon Shaikh Bashir has been elected President of the Republic of Lebanon. God help those who opposed him, unless he truly meant it when he promised 'understanding, democracy and justice for all Lebanese, Christians and Muslims alike.'

In the daytime, West Beirut was filled with the sound of bullets shot in farewell to the departing Palestinians. Now it is night, and West Beirut's destruction and pain are cloaked in darkness, while East Beirut rejoices at Shaikh Bashir's election by firing into the air and exploding dynamite. Six people were killed and seventeen were wounded by stray bullets in West Beirut; three were killed and eleven wounded by stray fire in East Beirut. Nothing has changed, the Lebanese are all the same.

Tuesday August 24th brings the miracle of miracles. Both electricity and water have been switched on for West Beirut. As the Palestinians continue to leave, the siege ends slowly. We prepare to roll out the 'Hi', 'Bonjour' and 'Ciao' and to see the Lebanese army again after a seven-year absence.

This morning Yasser Arafat handed the Lebanese army what was left of the PLO's heavy weapons in West Beirut: one mortar. 'Sharon claims that this is all that's left in West Beirut,' he said, 'so, as agreed, I am handing it over to you before we leave Lebanon.'

Beirut, I wrote this diary originally to ease my pain. Now it is to you I address myself. I love you East and West, North and

South. I love you when you laugh or cry, when you are dirty or clean, in darkness or lit up, when you have water and when you are without. I know you'll always be here, holding your head high unlike the rest of the Arab capitals. You and those who stayed are proof of courage in the face of savagery. From today on you deserve to live in honour and in peace.

CHAPTER 18

The last part is still to tell. Today is Monday August 30th. I woke up ten minutes after midnight, shaken to the core and screaming: 'Bombers, bombers!' It was pitch black outside and the only sound was that of the two Israeli bombers nearly scraping the roof. They were gone within seconds, but I couldn't go back to sleep. At five o'clock in the morning I still sat waiting for the next wave. They hadn't come back—maybe they weren't coming back.

I got up and prepared my coffee. Today was both sad and joyful, sad because Arafat was leaving West Beirut, joyful because he was alive in spite of everything. I put on my jeans and a T-shirt, and hurried over to Walid Joumblatt's house, where Arafat was going to give a press conference. By eight in the morning journalists and cameramen were stepping on each other's toes. There were armed elements everywhere. Some of the people who had come to listen were downcast, others were merely curious, and still others were in tears.

I thought Rasha must be happy: Abou Ammar was fine. I wondered if she knew he was leaving today. Probably not, as I had been told she refused to listen to the news and stolidly ignored every air raid on Beirut.

Since June 4th, 1982, 17,825 people have been killed and 30,103 wounded—nearly five people for every square kilometre of Lebanon. These people protected you, Arafat, and you were worth protecting as the symbol of a just cause. You moved from building to building and each was hit in turn, from shelter to shelter and each received its share of phosphorus bombs. But the Israelis failed to mow down the head of the PLO.

At nine o'clock Arafat arrived in full battle-dress, wearing the black-and-white checked Palestinian *keffiyeh*, which his men had wound around their helmets. People clapped in rage, frustration and joy. I could barely see through the crowd. The whole National Movement had turned out to bid him farewell. Suddenly tears blinded me and I angrily brushed them away.

Two days ago Arafat had gone to say goodbye to Saeb Salam and his wife Tamima. He kissed her hand and said: 'I salute the women who stayed and helped in the siege and battle of West Beirut. I will never be able to express my thanks.'

You have, Arafat, without knowing it: you taught us how to endure and to be patient. You protected us as we protected you. Of all the Arab leaders, you are the only real head of state although you have no country.

At Walid Joumblatt's, the two men tried in vain to maintain a brave front. 'I'm glad my father [assassinated leader and deputy Kamal Joumblatt] is not here to see this day,' Walid Joumblatt said. 'It is partly your father's death that led to this moment,' Arafat answered bitterly. The show of bravado kept cracking; the wan smiles and niceties served to no avail. I felt a surge of anger and despair: Arafat might be going out alive but we were defeated, utterly beaten. No, I refused to think that way: the Israelis didn't make it into the heart of West Beirut.

Arafat stood up to leave, and I sobbed my heart out as the women threw rice in a last gesture of farewell. I cried for our lost Arab nationalism, the indifference of the Arab world, the thought of the Israelis at Beirut Airport. I cried for the 17,825 dead, the orphaned children, the widows, all the misery and pain, for the Palestinian people setting out on their fourth exodus with their heads held high.

I pulled myself together and followed the procession as the crowd followed him to pay his last respects to Prime Minister Chafic Wazzan, who was accompanying him to the Greek ship waiting in Beirut's port. Two American vessels and one French naval ship were to escort him to Greece, where he was being met by Prime Minister Andreas Papandreou.

The traffic at Wazzan's offices disturbed me—we had got used to empty streets. A policeman we all knew tried to pull his weight ordering us to stand on one side. 'Where were you in the last three months?' I asked jokingly, and got a sheepish smile and permission to stay where I wanted. Those who stayed in West Beirut felt strange; it was difficult to communicate with those who weren't here during the siege.

The siege should be over today, when the last of the Palestinians leave.

We drove down to the harbour to get there before Arafat; it looked like something out of an old film about Berlin in 1945. It was an eerie feeling. We had to stop the car and go on by foot; there was sand everywhere and huge mounds of refuse. We walked under the scorching sun and could just see a glimpse of a very blue and calm Mediterranean sea between the piles of dirt.

There was a crumbling wall to our right. I stopped and looked at it as if I was in a dream: where had I seen that wall before? My memory fumbled for the answer and I felt faint. I had recognised it: it was the graveyard where my mother was buried. My life passed before my eyes, not a grand and glorious life, but that of a misfit and a failure.

I saw myself standing on that balcony in Jaffa overlooking Tel Aviv; I was six, but did not stay long. That same year, I was in another town in Palestine, Tulkarm, with hundreds of cannons blasting away around me. Fire and hatred mingled. Then Damascus, and the air raids, and I lay in bed, a small girl screaming her head off as she saw a building crumble; she was covered in shattered glass and no one came to pick her up; everyone was in the shelters. Why wasn't that little girl picked up?

Then Lina in Beirut: a happy-go-lucky girl who did well at school and never cheated (only twice at ages eight and ten). A dying mother in 1957, and suddenly four children, three brothers and one sister, left without that protective cocoon. A civil war in Lebanon in 1958—knives and guns were used, a little war. A home destroyed; father and two brothers wounded by a time bomb. Then on to an honours degree in 1962, and being voted most popular girl in the class. An Alice-in-Wonderland summer in sixteenth-century surroundings in Portugal, mingling with the royalty of Europe. Then back to reality, with a face for the world that laughed and hid the pain inside. From then on, a jack-of-all trades: secretary to the Libyan Ambassador, hostess at the Lebanese pavilion at the New York World Fair, researcher at the Lebanese Foreign Ministry, journalist, actress, writer, guide at the United Nations, holder of a Master's degree, wife, mother, sister. A misfit, a flop.

I stood before the tombs desecrated by bombs and thought:

I have one accomplishment; I lived through the siege of Beirut and survived.

People suddenly started screaming and pushing from all sides: a car passed through the army barricades and into the port area; you could barely see the car for all the armed men around it.

'Who was that?' I asked.

'Arafat!'

'Allah ma'ak, Allah ma'ak [God go with you],' I screamed at the top of my voice—everybody heard me except Arafat!

A page is turned, a new one begins. The siege of Beirut is about to be lifted. According to UN figures, 6,775 people were killed and 29,912 wounded in West Beirut alone. There is food now, and electricity, a bit of water, fuel and gas.

Will there be peace?

EPILOGUE

It is five o'clock in the morning of September 13th—21 days after the election of Bashir Gemayel, 14 days after the departure of the last Palestinian and Syrian fighters from Beirut. Today, I am leaving too; my suitcase is packed and so is my cousin's apartment in case she comes back before I do. I'm going to Damascus by road with friends. I had been waiting for the airport to open, but in vain.

I am tired and need the rest, but leaving hurts. My daughter Rasha is back in Beirut; she came down from Doha ten days ago. Leyla decided to wait and see what was going to happen first, and stayed with her aunt in Doha. I give myself a shake: maybe when I'm on the plane from Damascus to Paris I'll get over this feeling of anxiety. The telephone rings.

'Lina, there's a bit of bombing at Dahr al-Baidar on the road to Damascus.'

'So? What time are you coming to pick me up?'

'You still want to go in spite of the bombing?'

'Sure, it should be over by the time we're there.'

There are four of us in the car, riding in total silence. The difference between West and East Beirut is astounding: on one side, total destruction; on the other, life continues normally. It is too early for traffic jams, but the cars on the road stop us long enough to read the signs in Hebrew posted all over the place. I make no comment: my eyes are riveted on the letters and I feel cold and apprehensive. I wish I hadn't come after all; I was better off in my little corner of West Beirut.

'Brace yourselves, this is it!'

There's a checkpoint right in front of us. A Lebanese checks our identity cards and motions us through. Ten metres away from him stands an Israeli soldier, who is telling all the cars to go back where they came from. He barely looks at us when our turn comes and waves us on.

'What does that mean?'

'Go, go, he's telling you to go through. Oh, for God's sake move on before he changes his mind.'

'Why is he letting us through?'

'Why not?'

'Everybody else has been sent back.'

'I guess we're lucky.'

We move on slowly, barely believing our luck. We hadn't been searched or asked any questions, and only one Israeli had stopped us.

'My God, look at those roads.'

'You call these roads? There must have been a hell of a fight here.'

By 6.50 in the morning we've nearly reached Dahr al-Baidar. It really is too good to be true. There are Syrian checkpoints every fifty metres now—not one of them stops us. What a difference between these and the ones we had in Ainab five years ago.

'Which way do I go?'

'To your right. What's this?'

'What's what?'

'There, in front of you.'

A huge mushroom of smoke rises in the sky, right before our eyes.

'That's Dahr al-Baidar. Let's ask the Syrians.'

'Oh come on, let's move on.'

'No, no, please stop and ask,' I beg frantically as I see two other mushrooms forming, 'Oh please stop.'

At the Syrian checkpoint, the soldier tells us from behind his sandbags, 'The Israelis are bombing Dahr al-Baidar. You may be able to get through to the Lebanese border if you hurry.'

141

Hurry? Now I can hear the bombers, and I feel numb. I had nearly forgotten what they sounded like, but my memory quickly returns.

'Well, what do we do now?' the driver asks coolly. He has just returned from Saudi Arabia and hasn't experienced the war; the jets don't impress him.

'Don't just stand there,' shouts a Syrian soldier who is running for his life, 'There is a Syrian base right next to you.'

'Jesus Christ, let's get out of here,' I say, weak with fear.

Six hours later, we're still stuck there, and the bombing hasn't stopped for a minute. One road is completely destroyed, and the Israelis have closed their checkpoint. No one can go forward, and no one can go back through the Syrian checkpoint. I am almost hysterical.

'Shall we try the Tarshish road?'

We try, but we don't get very far when we see at first hand what a phosphorus bomb does when it explodes. You must try it sometime, then you can say you've tried everything. First you hear a noise that sounds like the cracking of a whip, then whoosh. . . and all you can see is the biggest bonfire ever. I scream my head off and start praying. To think that we have survived the siege of Beirut to come and die in this God-forsaken place.

At 5.30 in the evening we were still there, 247 air raids later. The fog that came down and gave us a brief respite has lifted again, taking hope with it.

'Let's go back to Beirut,' I say tonelessly.

We can't go back the way we came, so we go through Bikfaya, Gemayel's home town. I haven't been there since I visited his sister Arze twenty years ago. The town's shops all sport pictures of Shaikh Bashir, like the houses and the streets all the way down to East Beirut. Here shops are open, and everybody is wearing the latest fashions. The women are all tanned while we look like aspirins. We cross into West Beirut through the Museum, and I stare at all the destroyed buildings. I won't forget Monday September 13th very easily. I thought I was tired this morning; now there are no words to describe how I feel.

'Would you like to try again tomorrow?'

'Are you kidding? I am going nowhere tomorrow except bed. I'll try on Wednesday, by taxi and through Tripoli, that should be a safer road.' We'd seen a bridge blown away before our eyes, we'd seen the wounded being carried away on stretchers, we'd had a closer look at the Israeli jets. I've had enough.

I sleep like a log that night. No one knows I am back so no one disturbs me. And I'm too tired to go through the agony of saying goodbye to Rasha once more, so I stay in bed all of Tuesday. It is lovely outside, and the sky is very blue—not what it was like a week ago when an armed group clashed with the Lebanese army and hit an ammunition-packed truck belonging to the multinational forces. Then the sky had been black for twenty-four hours, buildings were destroyed and glass that had been replaced was shattered again.

Today is peaceful. All is quiet outside and the citizens of West Beirut are busy repairing their houses before winter comes—those who have houses left, that is. Schools reopen on November 4th, and they must get ready before then. The price of glass, wood and cement has soared; I am sure we will have another group of nouveaux-riches when this war is over, like we did after the last one. The war is over, isn't it? The army has taken over all the checkpoints that separate East and West, which were willingly ceded by the various organisations in the National Movement. This was all accomplished with great fanfare and amidst scenes of hugging and kissing. The only road that remains to be reopened is the ring-road, and that is supposed to be ready for reopening tomorrow morning at a great ceremony that will be presided over by the Prime Minister. The front is quiet and I'm sure I can leave tomorrow without any problems.

The doorbell brings me out of my reverie. It is Anne-Marie, my childhood friend. She has come to see how I'm doing, and looks at the suitcase I left packed by the door questioningly. I explain what happened, and we talk and talk through the evening about everything and nothing. At one point she remembers something:

'Turn the radio on.'

'Why? Has something happened?'

'I don't know exactly what it is,' Anne-Marie says, 'but I've heard there was an explosion at the Phalangists' headquarters in Ashrafiye.'

'That's impossible,' I exclaim, 'I would have heard it and I haven't left the house all day.' In a top storey in West Beirut you can clearly hear explosions or shooting in the East, particularly in my area.

The radio confirms Anne-Marie's story, but gives no more details. After she leaves, I turn the TV on. The newscaster looks white and stunned: we are told that Shaikh Bashir was in the building, that he escaped death by a miracle, and that he even managed to say a few words to those who stood outside before he helped to dig out the wounded. The announcer gives no other details and there are no pictures of the incident. At 8.30 in the evening, the news is exactly the same. All I can think of is that I didn't hear any explosion in the afternoon. At ten o'clock I go to sleep, only to be awakened by the phone at one in the morning.

'Lina, it's Sarah. I heard you were leaving for Damascus tomorrow.'

'So they say,' I answered sleepily.

'I just wanted to tell you that Shaikh Bashir is dead.'

'Who?'

'Shaikh Bashir Gemayel.'

'What do you mean, he's dead? He was fine yesterday evening or so the news told us.'

'Will you still leave tomorrow?'

'I'm not going anywhere!'

What other catastrophes await us? Is Beirut's nightmare ever going to be over? I ask myself this question hundreds of times on Wednesday while I watch Bashir Gemayel's funeral on television. I spend the day with Rasha, while everybody who's anybody, both enemy and ally, goes to the funeral in Bikfaya or sends a cable of condolences. Unity at a funeral—how ironic.

The citizens of East Beirut are inconsolable; those of West Beirut are subdued and holding their breath. You can read the fear in their eyes: what next? Many had high hopes of Shaikh Bashir after a meeting between him and Saeb Salam just four days ago which had gone very well and which seemed to set the stage for Muslim-Christian reconciliation.

Who killed Shaikh Bashir? That is a question nobody answers. The only thing that's certain is the fear in our hearts. At five in the evening we hear that the Israeli army is advancing through five fronts into West Beirut. I can't sleep because of the bombing; I can see the fires in the distance. I run from room to room as it gets closer. At five in the morning I sob my

144

heart out to Nadia in London. I'm sure it will be my last phone call. Three months of resistance for nothing: didn't I tell you that Sharon would not stop at the gates of West Beirut. My God, my God, they are barely seven hundred metres away from where I live. Most of those who fought are no longer here to protect us, and the National Movement has just finished giving most of its arms to the Lebanese army.

How can I write what I feel? I want to die, but I suppress this wish for death and, after dressing blindly, I run over to Rasha's house to protect her. She laughs at the sight of me:

'You look awful, Mummy.'

'I need a drink.'

'It's only half-past eight!'

'It doesn't matter. I need a drink and a valium.' I am cracking up. I try to ignore the bombing, and go from room to room to look for a good hiding place. Finally, I settle down in Leyla's room. Leyla was right to wait and see before she came back. 'Mummy, this isn't a very good hiding place, you're right by the window.' I am out of my mind with panic.

'There is a shelter where I live,' I say to Nabil, who is sitting there calm and collected. 'Can I take Rasha there?' He says yes, although it isn't safe to move outside. I later find out the Israelis shot first and asked questions later; it is a good thing I don't know it at the time. I take Rasha and Fatima and we hurry off frantically. The gate is locked. 'Open up, open up!' I scream. People are hiding everywhere; behind the gates they look like prisoners behind bars. Every face is frozen in fear.

'Where are they?'

'Very close to here. Open up!'

Rasha looks around the shelter in bewilderment; Fatima sits on the floor, and I pace up and down. I feel such shame: God, let them come and get it over with. I hear the spurts of a kalashnikov from time to time; each bullet is answered by a rocket or a bomb. A few hours later the radio announces that the Israelis have reached Sanayeh, the place where I live, the heart of West Beirut. Rasha is bored, Fatima is asleep, and I am still standing almost at attention.

Every once in a while there is an explosion and glass shatters all around; the electricity restored a few days ago has been cut off again. That night, when silence falls over Beirut, I take

Rasha home and see no one on the streets, nothing but burnt-out cars and debris. The window I had hidden under earlier is broken, the glass carpeting the ground. I put Rasha to bed and sleep next to her in my clothes; I hold her close and feel that she protects me.

The next morning, I stand on the balcony at dawn, with tears of rage and frustration in my eyes at the sight of two young men helping the Israelis set up a barricade two hundred metres away. I look at the piles of kalashnikovs and khaki outfits that have been dumped on the garbage heaps in the street—piles that will later explode when they are set on fire. I want to scream at the young men, to cry, to do something. I go home and take a bath. I come back and pick up Rasha, and from then on she is my protection against what is happening around us, she and her three little girlfriends. They are with me from nine in the morning to six in the evening; the only time I'm human is when I serve then lunch and dinner and talk to them.

'Mummy, please don't cry, don't cry.' This is all I can do most of the time.

I hear of collaborators who have already emerged; one in our neighbourhood was seen parading in an Israeli uniform before his neighbours' and friends' astounded gaze. I envy the dead; I wish I were with them. My hands shake all the time; vodka is like water to me now; four packets of cigarettes a day are barely enough. Is there more to come? I can't bear to think of the humiliation of it all. Wherever I go, I take Rasha with me. She points out which are the Lebanese army barricades and reassures me. I don't know what she's saying: have the Israelis withdrawn? I don't know anything anymore; days and nights are one long nightmare. What day are we? What month?

In the meantime, the Israelis are having a field-day in the occupied Arab capital. The spoils of war, they tell me. Books, documents, cars are carted away; trucks carry away the contents of supermarkets; even the French cultural centre is emptied. Old archives, maps and books disappear.

My neighbour tells me there's alarming news. What more can happen? Is it possible there could be more tragedy? It seems twenty truckloads of Lebanese armed elements were seen at the airport. I can't sleep tonight, and pray for death; it's so much better than this humiliation and self-disgust.

An abyss of despair gapes before us: there has been a massacre at Sabra and Chatila, the two Palestinian refugee camps near the airport, which the Palestinian fighters left unarmed, trusting to American guarantees. The number of massacred men, women and children is unknown; estimates range between 600 and 3,200. Does the number matter? I still feed and care for Rasha, but she can't protect me any more. I cannot stop crying, but this is different; my sobs are like a man's, harsh and without tears. I look at myself from afar, as if I were two different people, one warily observing the other. Am I human? Are those outside human or beasts? Animals care more about each other. Will I ever stop crying?

Anne-Marie is here, to ask me if I want to go for a drive. I look at her helplessly; I haven't gone out, slept or eaten for a long, long time. 'Do you feel like attending the mass funeral?' she asks. We go out. Just a few days ago, I passed through these streets on the way back from Damascus and commented at the destruction on the way; it was nothing to what there is now. But I don't say anything, just look silently.

'They're savages,' I mutter.

Anne-Marie says nothing. She just drives on doggedly, ignoring the Israeli presence. I look at them in a detached way as if they don't exist.

In Sabra, I stand next to the survivors and look at the ditch. I can see three little heads on a stretcher. 'God damn you Arabs,' a man screams after he's checked and rechecked the identity of a woman and child lying together—his wife and six-year-old son. What had the Arabs to do with this? Why doesn't he curse the Israelis who have massacred by proxy? Why not the Americans and their worthless guarantees? Why not the multinational forces who were here but who left before their mandate was up? Can this man believe in humanity any more? Can anyone?

I don't know. I know nothing. I'm not even bothered by the smell, though it will remain with me forever. 'Do you know they cut a baby up and fried him?' one man says. Can it be true? Would praying help? It doesn't.

'Let's go, Anne-Marie, let's go. There's nothing we can do, here or anywhere else.' I am dry-eyed at last.

I need another drink. What I don't need is to listen to the news: that Shaikh Amin Gemayel, Shaikh Bashir's brother, has been elected President unanimously by Christians and Muslims alike; that the multinational forces are coming in again to protect us; that the Israelis have started to withdraw; that the Lebanese army is taking over.

They tell me 'Operation Peace for Galilee' is over. It seems I have survived this magnificent peace—or have I?

I take Rasha and her friends out on a tour of West Beirut.

'Mummy, what did you feel when you saw all the destroyed buildings?' Rasha asks.

'Nothing. And you?'

'I cried.'

How can I ever thank you Menahem Begin, and you Ariel Sharon, and you Rafael Eitan and Yitzhak Shamir; and you Hitler? And all you Arabs with your indifference, and you Americans? Thank you for having turned my nine-year-old child into an adult overnight.

My love and my thanks go to my cousin Nadia, who sustained me during my most difficult moments; this book I owe to her and her help.

CHRONOLOGY

Publisher's note: This chronology is provided to give readers an easy reference to the Arab-Israeli conflict and its repercussions in Lebanon.

1864   Mount Lebanon becomes autonomous Christian province under the Ottoman Empire

1897   First Zionist Congress, held in Basle, declares the aim of Zionism is to 'create for the Jewish people a home in Palestine secured by public law'

1898   Jewish Colonial Trust and Colonisation Commission set up by the Zionists

1901   Jewish National Fund set up by the Zionists

1908   Palestine Office and Palestine Land Development Company set up by Zionists. Jews were still under eight per cent of the population of Palestine, owning 2.5 per cent of the land

1914   World War I: Turks join in on Germany's side

1915   Letters between Sherif Hussein of Mecca and British High Commissioner in Egypt, Sir Henry McMahon, promise Arabs independence in return for help against the Turks

1916   Secret British-French agreement (Sykes-Picot) divides Ottoman Empire into spheres of control

1917   British Foreign Secretary Arthur Balfour declares Britain 'views with favour the establishment in Palestine of a National Home for the Jewish people'

1919   Paris Peace Conference: mandate system decided for Arab provinces of Ottoman Empire; Zionists submit plan for Jewish control of Palestine which includes South Lebanon and Litani River

1920   Britain assumes mandatory control of Palestine and Trans-Jordan (the latter is excluded from terms of Balfour Declaration); France assumes mandatory control of Lebanon and Syria, adds some Muslim areas of Syria to Mount Lebanon to make Greater Lebanon

1936   Protests of Palestine Arabs against British rule and Zionist immigration culminate in general strike and all-out rebellion

1939   World War II begins

1942   Zionists meeting in New York Biltmore Hotel call for establishment of Jewish commonwealth in Palestine, unrestricted immigration and setting up of Jewish military force

1943   Zionist Organisation calls for sovereign Jewish state and eventual transfer of Palestinian Arabs to Iraq

        Lebanon declares its independence from France; draws up National Covenant, the unwritten 'gentleman's agreement' by which government is based on confessional system; the president to be a Maronite Christian, the prime minister a Sunni Muslim, and the parliament speaker a Shia Muslim

1947	United Nations recommends partition of Palestine into Jewish and Arab states; 50 per cent of the best land to go to the Jews who will still own only 5.67 per cent; Arabs reject plan
	Jewish militias in Palestine increase attacks against both British and Arabs
1948	Massacre of Palestinian Arabs at Deir Yassin by Menahem Begin's Stern Gang spreads panic among Arab population, provoking many to flee
	British mandate ends; Jews declare state of Israel in all areas under their control; neighbouring Arab states send in armies but are defeated; 400,000 Palestinians seek refuge in neighbouring states
1949	Israel signs armistice agreements with Egypt, Lebanon, Jordan and Syria; total number of refugees reaches 750,000; UN Relief and Works Agency (UNRWA) set up to cope
1950	Lebanon refuses economic union with Syria; economic recession results
	Palestinian refugees in Lebanon settle in 15 permanent camps throughout the country
1952	Camille Chamoun elected President of Lebanon in September
1956	Britain, France, Israel invade Suez, withdraw under US pressure
1957	Lebanon accepts US aid under Eisenhower Doctrine
1958	Chamoun suspected of trying to extend his presidency; civil war breaks out; US marines land in July to restore order; Fuad Chehab elected President of Lebanon in September; US troops leave in October
1964	Arab League set up Palestine Liberation Organisation (PLO)
	Charles Helou elected President of Lebanon
1965	Fateh (the Palestine National Liberation Movement) launches its first guerrilla operation against Israel on January 1st
1967	The Six-Day war breaks out on June 5th: Israel defeats Egypt, Syria and Jordan, and occupies the Sinai, the Golan Heights, the Gaza Strip and the West Bank; 200,000 more Palestinians flee to neighbouring states
1968	Guerrilla operations increase from Jordan and Lebanon; Palestinian groups attack Israeli interests abroad; Israel retaliates against Jordan and Lebanon and in December bombs Beirut Airport destroying 13 planes
1969	Guerrillas take over PLO; tension develops between Palestinians and governments in Lebanon and Jordan
	Cairo Agreements signed in November to regulate Palestinian activity in Lebanon, giving them freedom of movement in South
1970	Jordanian Army attacks Palestinian guerrillas in September killing thousands and expelling the rest, many of whom go to Lebanon
	Suleiman Franjiye elected President of Lebanon in August,

appoints Saeb Salam premier; Israeli attacks on Lebanon and Palestinian guerrillas increase

1973   Egypt and Syria attack Israel in October War (known in Israel as Yom Kippur War), Egypt regains Suez Canal; Arab oil embargo imposed

1974   PLO Chairman Yasser Arafat addresses UN General Assembly in November

1975   Saudi King Feysal assassinated in March
Lebanese civil war begins in April; Palestinians are drawn in on Muslim-leftist side

1976   Elias Sarkis elected President of Lebanon in May, with Syrian backing; in June 6,000 Syrian troops enter Lebanon, support Christian-rightist side in civil war
Two-month siege of Palestinian refugee camp of Tal al-Zaatar by Christian-rightist forces; 1,000 Palestinians are massacred as they leave the camp
Arab League arranges ceasefire in October; Syrian forces increased to 25,000 as part of Arab peacekeeping force in Lebanon

1977   Menahem Begin elected premier in Israel in May
Syrian relations with Lebanese Christian-rightists deteriorate by August
Egyptian President Anwar Sadat goes to Jerusalem in November
Arab states rejecting Egyptian-Israeli talks form Confrontation and Steadfastness Front in Tripoli (consists of Syria, Iraq, Libya, Algeria, South Yemen and the PLO)

1978   Israel invades South Lebanon in March, withdraws after US pressure in June; area patrolled by United Nations Interim Force in Lebanon (UNIFIL), except for border area which Israel hands over to renegade Lebanese Army Major Saad Haddad
In September Egypt, Israel reach Camp David Accords under US auspices
In November Arab states hold summit in Baghdad, decide to suspend Egypt from Arab League if it signs separate treaty

1979   In March Egypt, Israel sign peace treaty under Camp David Accords, begin 'autonomy' talks for Palestinians in West Bank and Gaza; Arabs boycott Egypt
Saad Haddad declares his area 'Independent Free Lebanon' in April

1980   Bashir Gemayel (son of Phalangist Party founder Pierre Gemayel) leads his militia against rival Christian militia of Dany Chamoun (son of Camille Chamoun) and wins overall control of Maronite areas under 'Lebanese Forces'

1981   Israel begins heavy attacks on South Lebanon in April; following Israeli-Palestinian battles, US special envoy Philip Habib arranges ceasefire in July; Palestinians cease all border operations from Lebanon
President Sadat assassinated in October

1982   Attempted assassination of Israel's ambassador in London in June; Israel invades Lebanon, reaching Beirut and placing the city under siege; PLO evacuates Beirut in August; Lebanese president-elect Bashir Gemayel assassinated in September, Israeli forces enter West Beirut; Palestinians massacred in Sabra and Chatila refugee camps

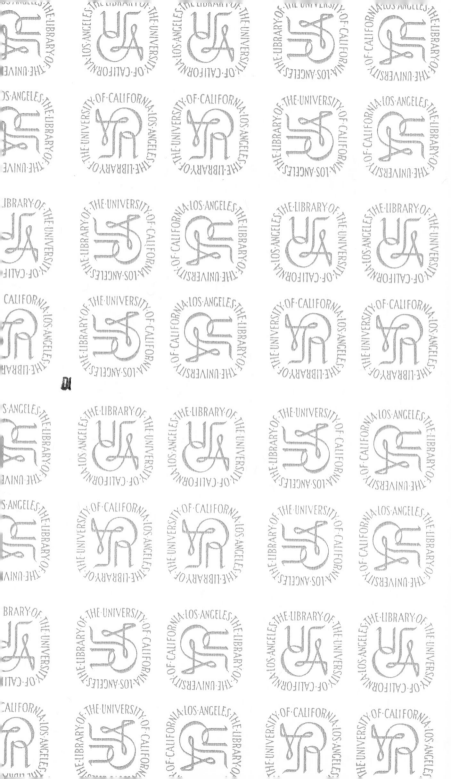